I OWE RUSSIA $1200

I OWE RUSSIA $1200

BOB HOPE

DOUBLEDAY & COMPANY, INC.

GARDEN CITY, NEW YORK

LIBRARY OF CONGRESS CATALOG CARD NUMBER 63–10519
COPYRIGHT © 1963 BY BOB HOPE

IN THE MEMORY OF
JACK HOPE
MY BROTHER
MY PRODUCER
MY FRIEND

ACKNOWLEDGMENT

The photographs in this book came from many sources. Special thanks are due to NBC for permission to use photographs by Paul Bailey, Herb Ball, and Gerald K. Smith; also to *Look* magazine; to United Artists; to Paramount Pictures; to Metro-Goldwyn-Mayer; and to the others whose names appear with the photographs.

PREFACE

When Soviet Cosmonaut Andrian G. Nikolayev stepped out of his capsule, he had gone 64 times around the world. He almost tied my record. And I did it the hard way—tourist!

People ask me, "Why do you keep moving so much?" My stock answer is, "With my kind of act, it's safer."

Somewhere high in my family tree, I must have had a relative who was a mule-skinner for Marco Polo, or a gypsy dancer, or a Pullman porter—or maybe it's because my mother put jet fuel in my Pablum.

They say every comedian wants to play Shakespeare but I have the distinction of being the only comedian Shakespeare talked about! His "All the world's a stage" could only have been a sly reference to my extensive journeys in search of a captive audience as set down in this book. It's all been one stage, all right, whether the setting was an aircraft carrier in the Bay of Naples or a snowbank in Thule, Greenland, or the well-"bugged" hall in our Embassy in Moscow, because the producer and director was always Uncle Sam. I won't work for anyone else.

This book, of course, consists of recollections of the recent past. Now what about the future? What trips, events, people, or jokes will inspire my next literary opus? I can hardly wait to find out.

Will I be picked to entertain a company of bored astronauts on the moon (with a quick stop at the space station for a cup of radioactive coffee and a few hilarious ad-libs)? Of course, I'll go if I'm asked but truthfully, Venus sounds more like my room. It has an atmosphere, you know.

7

The only drawback there would be if I arrived and found out they celebrate Christmas in July and I'd be stuck with a lot of great material. Also they'd have to send a monkey to Venus first and I don't know if I can follow Enos.

Incidentally, this book is being rushed into print in the hope that you'll read it while you're still on this planet. That sounds a little wild, but who knows—this narrative may be reviewed by a little green man with antennae growing out of his head and one big eye in the middle of his forehead.

Seriously, it's fascinating to reflect on the future, which seems to have arrived already with Telstar. Telstar has brought people on Earth infinitely closer together and should yield remarkable results. Imagine the whole world maintaining the same suds level, decreasing tooth cavities by 22 per cent, and eliminating under-arm perspiration—all the time singing along with Mitch? Telstar is a tremendous advance in communications. It's the greatest scientific achievement ever to appear on your phone bill.

Yes, the conquest of space is within our grasp, but as we reach out we seem to have diminished the inward search. No significant breakthrough has yet been made in the art of human relations. So perhaps this is the precise moment in history for each of us to look into his heart and his conscience and determine in what way we may be responsible for our present dilemma. I have examined mine—and at this time I should like to make a confession. I owe Russia twelve hundred dollars. How I happen to owe them twelve hundred dollars is a long story. In fact, I intend to get a book out of it.

I OWE RUSSIA $1200

Me, Mrs. Khrushchev, and my favorite three iron.

CHAPTER ONE

You know how to start a cold war?

Sit next to Mrs. Khrushchev at a luncheon and casually say, "Why don't you visit Disneyland? All the tourists go there." Then have Frank Sinatra say, "Yeah, you gotta make that scene . . . I'll take you." Then Mrs. K. says, "That sounds like a wonderful idea. I'll ask Nickie."

That's the way it all happened the day Spyros Skouras gave the now famous luncheon for Nikita Khrushchev. Nikita was thrilled about coming to lunch at 20th Century-Fox. He thought the studio was named after him.

Mrs. Khrushchev was seated between Frankie and me and we were just trying to keep a polite conversation going which wasn't easy when everything had to be shouted through an interpreter. I had picked what seemed the most innocent topic in the world. Mrs. K. was fascinated by the idea of Disneyland and she wrote a note and passed it to her husband who was staring down at us from the head table where he was seated with Eric Johnson, Mr. Skouras, Henry Cabot Lodge, and other State Department officials.

Nikita read the note, nodded in agreement, and whispered to his Number One man to fix a trip to Disneyland. He was sitting there beaming in anticipation of his first ride on the Whirling Tea Cups and a visit to Tom Sawyer Island when the aide returned and whispered to him, "The Los Angeles Security Police will not allow you to make the trip."

A little steam came out of Nikita's head. He took off his shoe, tapped for silence, and said, "Fine country! You invite me to eat with you but you won't let me go to Disneyland. What kind of missiles are you building there?" We quickly found out why Mr. K. is known as "the fastest mouth alive." He took off on a ten-minute tantrum about the capitalist plot against his visiting Disneyland. Personally, I think they should have let him go to Disneyland—after all, he missed Congress.

That was the first time I had actually triggered a diplomatic incident with Mr. K. in the flesh. However, my private cold war with the Russians started a year earlier.

I was in London for the opening of *Paris Holiday*, a frothy little French pastry which went a million dollars over budget, but more about this wine break later. One night, while driving by Albert Hall, I noticed a line of people that must have numbered two thousand fighting to buy tickets. This annoyed me because I wasn't playing there.

The billboard listed something called the "Ukraine State Dance Ensemble." I might as well confess that I have always been an aficionado of the dance; the Lido girls, the June Taylor Dancers, and Rosita and Her Doves. This is art.

You can imagine my surprise when I looked up at the stage and a hundred and ten Goliaths came marching out. I'd have sneaked out, but they were carrying spears. That much I know about show business: Never walk out on an act that carries weapons.

I'm glad I didn't walk out. I enjoyed one of the most exciting evenings I'd ever had in a theatre. As I walked back to the hotel through the chill fog of the night, I was already on the road to Moscow.

Here was an entirely new facet of entertainment, new faces, new music, new acts. Here were people we were vitally involved with and yet knew little about. I had no master plan, no lofty concepts. I did not intend to solve any great problems. All I knew was that there was a tremendous, stimulating, different television show to be made in

Moscow. If there was a dent in the Iron Curtain, I was going to find it.

The next morning I led our little group to the Soviet Consulate at 5 Kensington Palace Gardens and we filed for our visas. Then I called Ursula Halloran, my P.R. in New York, and asked her to start working on it from the Washington end. And just to make sure, I called our NBC representative in Moscow, Irv Levine, and asked him to push from there.

I am not a patient man by nature, but in the next few months I became an authority on patience.

The first week the Consulate heard nothing. The second week they couldn't promise anything definite, but things were very encouraging. The third week we were back to the first week. The fourth week the man we had been talking to disappeared and we were informed he had never been there at all.

It was time to bring up the reserves. Like a typical tourist in need, I dialed the American Embassy in London and asked for my good friend Jock Whitney, our Ambassador to England. Jock promised nothing officially, but said he would be happy to raise the question that evening at a cocktail party where he expected to meet the Russian Ambassador, Jacob Malik. This he did, and Ambassador Malik, with a slow grin, asked, "What does your Mr. Hope want to do . . . entertain our troops in Red Square?"

Some day I hope they put him on TV opposite a good Western.

Time was growing short. In a few days I would have to return to New York. I checked with Ursula in New York. She was doing her best at the Russian Embassy. She was getting smiles but no visas.

I checked again with Irv Levine in Moscow. The Kremlin isn't the easiest place in the world from which to get information, but as far as Irv could tell, everything was going fine. Everybody approved. There just weren't any visas issued yet.

Then it hit me. It was all so easy. They couldn't push me around. "Irv," I shouted, "I'll fly to Copenhagen, buy a ticket on the Russian jet and climb aboard. Once I'm in Moscow, what can they do about it?"

There was a long pause at the other end of a rather noisy line. There seemed to be more clicking than usual. Then Irv answered. "It won't work, Bob. For two reasons. First, you can't get on a Russian airline without a visa. They're checked at the gate. And second, this telephone call is bugged."

My phone hung itself up.

I don't know if that phone call had anything to do with it, but Irv Levine is no longer our NBC representative in Moscow, by request of the Kremlin.

The press had been following our visa campaign carefully. When I packed to return to New York, this was duly noted. By the time I boarded the plane, my chagrin was ten pounds overweight.

For the next two weeks I worked personal appearances in New York and Florida. I didn't get too many laughs. Usually nothing bugs me, but this one was a real let-down.

Everywhere I went the press queried me about the visa delay. I parried the best I could with: "I can't understand it. I gave the names of two Czars who would vouch for me."

"This is the last time I borrow Walter Winchell's passport."

"Maybe they're sore 'cause I lied about my occupation. I put down 'actor.'"

"It's a technical problem. My passport's okay, but my jokes have expired."

I was running out of ad-libs and time. In less than a week I had to be back on the Coast to start my next television show. Then the call came from Julian Goodman of NBC Washington. Our visas were waiting at the Russian Embassy.

All things come to those who wait, as Bing can testify.

Honest, she's my press agent, Ursula Halloran.

15

I flew to Washington and went directly to the palatial Soviet Embassy.

It said *Welcome* on the mat, but I had my doubts.

After endless months of delays, red tape, and disappointments, I was entitled to a king-size case of jitters. With a hand that shook like the morning after, I opened the door.

I was greeted by Mrs. Tamara Y. Mamedov, the Cultural Attaché. She smiled warmly and said, "Hello, you conqueror!"

"Conqueror?" I ad-libbed.

"Nobody has ever received a visa to Moscow this fast."

"But we've been waiting for weeks and weeks."

She paused for a moment and then, as though explaining to a small child, she said, "It all takes time, Mr. Hope. You want to go over and study us, we want to study you."

With that, she led me to the second floor where a press conference had been arranged. It was the first time in history that American reporters had been admitted to the second floor of the Russian Embassy. Regardless of what else happened on our trip, the Cultural Exchange had already done some good.

After the press conference, I sat with Madame Mamedov and several assistants and was briefed on how to act in Moscow. The wording was rather elaborate but the essence was quite simple. All my negotiations for Russian talent were to be conducted with the Russian government and not with the artist. All money was to be paid directly to the state, none to the artist.

I could never be happy under a system like that. I don't get to keep the money either, but at least I get to feel it on its way to Washington.

We discussed my plans at length. I explained that I was not interested in anything political but wanted to see as much of Russian show business as possible. I wanted to meet their stars and artists and to see them perform. I wanted the freedom to film when and where I saw fit. I asked for sixteen visas. This would cover our production crew and ten film and sound technicians from England.

This was refused. The visas for the British film crew were denied and instead they "suggested" that a Russian film crew might serve better. Inasmuch as I couldn't operate a camera and be in front of it, I accepted this "suggestion."

In all I received six visas. One was for myself and two were for Arthur Jacobs and Ursula Halloran, my press representatives. The Russians were never the ones to underestimate the power of a good press.

The other three visas were to be issued in England. Two were for "The Owl and the Brush," that's Mort Lachman and Bill Larkin, my traveling writers, and the other one was for Ken Talbot, one of England's finest lighting-cameramen.

This was a pretty skinny crew with which to attempt an hour TV show, but, in retrospect, I guess we're lucky to have made it at all. Look at Art Linkletter. He tried for over a year to take his show to Russia and he's still waiting at the bus station.

Three days later we departed from International Airport in New York. Scandinavian Airlines was taking us to Copenhagen and a Russian jet would take us from there to Moscow.

I settled back in my seat. My passport was in my pocket. My briefcase with jokes was chained to my wrist. Once again the show was on the road and I was on my way to a place that for me was like the dark side of the moon.

Next stop Moscow, but there's been a lot of stops along the way. Let's talk about some of them first.

The space plumbers. (United Artists photo)

CHAPTER TWO

I spent the summer of 1961 in England making a movie. The movie was *The Road to Hong Kong* and naturally, I made it with my old celluloid confrère. Bing Crosby.

After all, what would a Road picture be without Bing? Much, much better, I'm sure!

But, as the producers, Mel Frank and Norman Panama, told me, "When it's a Road picture, the public expects to see both Hope and Crosby in it. It's a sort of tradition." Incredible as it seems, some moviegoers might be disappointed if old Lard Hips weren't in the picture!

I reluctantly agreed. "Okay," I said, "I'll carry the old boy through one more epic."

Frank and Panama looked surprised. "Funny," they said, "that's just what Bing said about *you!*"

So early August found me on the way to England. Don't ask me why we were making a picture called *The Road to Hong Kong* in England. I heard it was partly to save money, and partly because Bing loves watercress sandwiches. And as you know, anything Bing has a yen for, he gets!

But I was happy about the trip. I always look forward to visiting England. England occupies a warm spot in my affections. It was the scene of my greatest performance. I was born there.

Since we were going to be in England for three months, I took the family along. I felt I owed them a vacation. Tony's marks at college were good, Linda had been working hard teaching school, and Kelly and Norah were behaving fairly well. They hadn't set fire to their piano teacher in over a month.

And, of course, Dolores deserved the trip. It's not easy for her, being married to a comedian. Many's the night Dolores and I have sat in the living room watching Red Skelton and Bob Newhart, two of her favorites, and no matter how funny they are, she always keeps a straight face. If they get too screamingly funny for her to stand it, she excuses herself and leaves the room to laugh. That's what I call a perfect wife.

And there was another reason I decided to take the family to England with me. President Kennedy had just come out with a ruling that Americans could only buy a hundred dollars worth of goods in foreign countries tax free. That made it perfect—imagine the government stepping in and helping you keep the lid on the family budget?

So I said, "All right, kids, we're all going to Old Blighty." I knew the kids would stay under the hundred dollar limit out of respect to JFK, and if Dolores got any wild ideas of a spending spree, I could appeal to her on grounds of patriotism.

To make the trip as much of a vacation as possible, we went over by ocean liner, the last trip of the *Liberté*. It was hard to believe that in two months that beautiful liner would be a Japanese railroad.

There's nothing like an ocean voyage. It's five days away from the world, away from the telephone, away from everything. And it was a real test for the kids. Five days without television.

But they managed to survive, and in due course we arrived at Southampton. When we landed, the deck stewards and maids and waiters lined up, and it was a very moving scene. They were all holding their hands out, waiting to wave good-bye. At least, I think they were waiting to wave good-bye. I almost got away without tipping, then my admiral's hat fell off.

Of course, with the whole family along, the first problem to be faced in England was getting a house. You don't check a family of six into the Dorchester Hotel or the Savoy; ordering meals from Room Service for that size gang, in a week you'd run up a higher fuel bill than Cape Canaveral's.

I'd written our English agents about this, and they had everything ready for us. They'd rented a house in the country for us, at a place called Cranbourne Court, about twenty miles from London, between Windsor and Ascot. We drove out there, and it turned out to be more than just a house—it was one of the stately old homes of England. It was practically a castle. It was the kind of house Shakespeare would've lived in if Laurence Olivier had been doing his shows.

This estate had a croquet court, golf driving range, two greenhouses—and it had some nice features outside, too. It was set in the middle of acres and acres of rolling lawns. Finally Tony spoke up with what we all were thinking. "If it doesn't have a power mower," he announced, "we're through!"

A typical English butler awaited us at the front door, complete with tailcoat and gray sideburns. The butler, not the door. With him were a couple of footmen and a covey of English housemaids.

I drew the house agent aside. "Listen," I hissed in his ear, "what goes? I don't need all these servants. I brought my own work group." I indicated Dolores and the kids. The layout was much too big, I told him, for just one family.

"Oh," he said, "it's not for just one family. The Crosbys are sharing the house with you."

I turned to Dolores and said, "Quick—back to the boat!"

As it turned out, the arrangement worked out fine. My family and Bing and Kathy and their youngsters all got along very well together. I think Bing got a little the best of the deal. We split the grocery bill straight down the middle, and the way the food disappeared, I think Bing was secretly shipping CARE packages back to the states to Gary, Dennis, Lindsey, and Philip.

The butler took us on a tour of the house. It was a typical ancient English country home, 56 rooms and a bath. It was a strange kind of bath—it went all the way around the place. It was called a moat.

The moat would come in handy. It was a nice place for Bing to rinse a few things. Like old money, etc.

We straggled along behind the butler through long dark corridors. Dolores exclaimed at the drapes, and the kids loved the size of the rooms. Every one of them was big enough to hold a baseball game in. The living room was the cozy room in the house. It was only ninety feet long.

The paintings were what got me. The house was full of old paintings, portraits of the owner's ancestors all the way back to William the Conqueror, the original subdivider.

With all those forbidding faces staring at me, it was like being back at Paramount Studios, at a stockholders' meeting.

This wasn't the first time the place had been rented, the butler informed us as he showed us through bedrooms the size of the Coliseum. One of the early owners, the Duke of Ludsbury, used to rent out rooms to travelers. If they were of the upper class, of course. The hall had been sort of a motel for knights.

I'm giving you a fast description of it, but it was really a beautiful old place. Just like you see in British movies. Long, wide corridors, long rows of doors, high ceilings, even a suit of armor on the stair landing. The place was so British, I wouldn't have been surprised if the mice wore monocles.

We entered a huge room on the upper floor which the butler informed us was the nursery. "When the owner's family were all in residence," the butler informed us, "there were a dozen little ones running around in here."

I told him to keep his voice down. Bing and Kathy might be nearby, and I didn't want them to hear that.

All British castles and old country homes are supposed to be haunted. It's in the lease.

Our first night in the place, we all decided to sit up late and see if we could get a glimpse of the old hall's famous ghost. To help things along, we turned off the electric lights and sat in the gloomy main hall, lighted only by flickering candles.

It was a goose-pimply experience. At midnight, the bell in the castle tower began to chime. Then we heard metallic rattling in the hall. We all rushed out expecting to see a genuine full-fledged ghost clanking down the hall in shining armor. But we were disappointed. The clanking sound was the butler putting away the silver. With Americans renting the place, he was also required to count it.

During our stay, we never did see the ghost. But ghost or no ghost, the old house certainly didn't lack atmosphere. At night you could hear the ancient timbers creaking and groaning, and the wind would whistle and moan through the turret windows on the upper floors. And, after you'd tossed and turned for an hour trying to get to sleep, you could almost hear the voices of the long-departed dukes and lords whispering, "Yankees, go home!"

Even without the ghost, the old place was good for a thrill or two. One night I got in real late. I was sneaking along the upper corridor in the dark, and as I turned a corner, I got the shock of my life. There in front of me a figure in a flowing robe shimmered in the moonlight. But it wasn't a ghost, either. It was Bing in his flannel nightgown.

If there was one thing that fine old country house had, it was elbowroom. It was so spacious, days would go by without the members of one family even laying eyes on the other; at times we wouldn't even know the Crosbys were around, except for an occasional wail from the nursery.

And the baby didn't cry very much. Except occasionally when Bing would accidentally wake it during its nap. Bing was always tiptoeing through the nursery and we couldn't figure out why. The reason was, Bing kept his pin money in a talcum powder can in the linen closet. He figured it was safe there. If anyone tried to snatch it, Junior would act as a burglar alarm.

I said that the two families seldom met, but of course we all sat down to dinner together in the dining hall two or three nights a week. It was quite a sight, Crosbys on one side of the table and Hopes on the other. And the butler lurking in the background waiting to referee. It was like mealtime in a vaudeville boardinghouse. What a hungry mob—it's the first time I ever saw a turkey chicken out.

Bing and I took turns at being the head of the family. One night Bing would carve, the next time I would carve.

And those meals were an education. You know how most families say grace before a meal? Bing's group also sings a full chorus of "White Christmas." Naturally, they always got the most food. Who could eat after hearing that!

Each family not only had the other to contend with, we also had the servants. At home in America you can kid with the maid and she becomes like a member of the family. But that doesn't go in England. We didn't kid with the servants over there, because they were superior to us and they knew it. For instance, our butler was an elderly, very dignified man called "Pope." For at least forty years he'd been wearing a tailcoat and polished black shoes in the house, and all those years he'd buttled for some of the best people in England. You couldn't fool him, he instinctively knew what was class and what wasn't. He kept looking at me like I was a borderline case.

I tried to make a little character by telling him that I was born in England. He paused for a moment and then said quite confidentially, "Don't worry, sir. Your secret is

24

Two Shangri-La beatniks. That's the last time I go to Bing's tailor.
(United Artists photo)

safe with me." Even though I was careful to put a coat and tie on every time I went downstairs, he knew I was really the type of guy who sprawls around the house in slacks and a tee shirt and slippers.

After a couple of weeks of the coat-and-tie routine, I gave up. One day I got brave and ventured downstairs in an old sweater and pants. It was no use. The butler trapped me on the landing. He stared at me glacially, then he said, "Good morning." After an agonizing pause, he added regretfully, "sir." What could I do? I retreated to my room and put on a necktie and a tweed jacket that was so British it looked like it had been woven by Clive of India.

Think I'm exaggerating? I'm not. The servants in England are so dignified, they intimidate you. It's tough to say, "Shine these shoes and have 'em back in ten minutes" to a guy who looks like Commander Whitehead.

I was afraid to ask the butler for a second helping of chicken. I had a feeling that if I did, he'd take it up with Parliament.

And you could sense that Crosby's valet didn't approve of the way Bing dressed. It was understandable. He'd never seen a fifty-eight-year-old beatnik before.

In fact, when Bing first strolled in wearing a tam o' shanter, sandals and long, droopy sweater, the valet bowed and said, "Shall I draw your bath, your Ladyship?"

The first day, Bing and I tried to break the ice with the butler. Bing said, "I guess it's tough on you, after all your years serving the titled gentry, having to put up with us Yanks."

"Oh, I've had worse moments, sir," the butler replied, "I was at Dunkirk!"

Another time when the kids were sliding down the banister of the great staircase, I said to the housekeeper, "What do you really think of us?"

She said seriously, "If I ever hit the football pool, sir, I'll be happy to tell you!"

We stayed in England three months making the picture, and let me tell you, there's nothing like an English summer. There's nothing like it, except, possibly, an Alaskan winter. Spending a summer in England is like running a lighthouse in the Antarctic. We had every kind of weather in the book —rain, fog, snow, sleet, sunshine—and usually they all came on the same day. I used to think English men were silly, starting for work on a bright sunny morning with umbrellas and rubbers, but after the first week I not only adapted

Fred Flintstone and friend. (United Artists photo)

those measures, I also wore a raincoat that opened up into a canvas lifeboat.

Of course, that's exaggerating a little, too, but not as much as you may think. The English weather is tricky; it shifts faster than a bubble dancer with a slow leak. I got in dutch with the English for criticizing their weather on one visit. In fact, they got so riled up at my jokes about the London fog, they insisted on an apology. And I was going to appear on television and apologize, too, but I never got to the TV station because of a mishap. My taxicab got lost in the fog.

And I'm not kidding about that fog. It was always with us. Everything gets so damp over there, Macmillan spends fifty pounds a year just for mustache wax.

But living in England was a wonderful experience. Both families found themselves enjoying it. The people, with their good manners and their British cheeriness, were getting to us. We found ourselves becoming more British every day. Instead of "Good morning" we found ourselves saying "Cheerio" and "Pip pip."

Cranbourne Court was just a few miles from Ascot, site of the famous race track. The British seem to have a more social approach to gambling than we do, and one of *the* things to do on a Saturday afternoon is "to box it at Ascot." And they really do know how to lay it on. For the peasants they have pari-mutuel windows where one may wager for cash. But if you're going to mingle with the Uppertweed, you must have your own betting commissioner—that's sort of a bookie with a bowler. Cash is never mentioned. You merely mention the number of a horse that appeals to you. He commends your choice. The race is held in almost silence. There's no real cheering as we know it—although in an exceptionally exciting race there is enthusiastic breathing. After the race your betting commissioner engages you in casual conversation but there is no mention of anything quite as rude as money. If you win you receive a cheque by

Madame Tussaud's parts department. That's my agent taking ten per cent off the top.

post thirty days later, if you lose you receive a black-bordered chit and a tranquilizer. It's all completely off-hand. It isn't whether you win or lose that counts, it's how you underplay your suicide.

We had a couple of great Saturday afternoons out there and Bing was outstanding, also veddy English in his pearl-gray topper and sport jacket.

Eleanor Harris, the magazine feature writer, stopped in to visit us on her way back from a trip to Russia with Jack Paar. We took her to Ascot with us one Saturday afternoon and she loved it. Just before the big race of the day I announced that I was going down to my betting commissioner to bet heavily on the favorite. It was my bet of the year— I was chucking all my loose pounds on Pandora. This horse was the cinch of the day—all the wise money was going this way and the odds were backed down to two to one. Eleanor looked in the form and asked me to bet a pound on a horse called Gold Daddy which was 30 to 1. A typical woman's bet, something for nothing, no savvy, no feel for the inside.

When I got to the betting commissioner, I was too embarrassed to even mention a one-pound wager. I was trying to give the impression that I was an English relative of Nick the Greek. So with my sure instinct in these matters I decided to book Eleanor's bet myself. I don't have to tell you the finish. My horse, Pandora, sagged in the gate. The only time she got to the rail was to lean on it. Eleanor's horse Gold Daddy ran like there was a talent scout for a dog food company in the stands.

I paid Eleanor, rather grimly, the posted odds 30 to 1, and she left for an appointment. Later the true odds were posted 24 to 1. I'm embarrassed about asking her for the six pounds back—it would be petty and small and unlike me. However, if she does read this and her conscience bothers her . . .

We had a lot of trouble getting to the studio. On the way we had to pass three or four of the most beautiful golf courses in the world: Sunningdale, Wentworth, the Berkshire, and the very exclusive Swinley Forest, which is the ultimate in posh. It's so exclusive, some of the members can't get in.

And the British are so eloquent. The first time I teed off at Swinley, I took a full swing at the ball, then heard one of the members say, "Never before has so much swung so hard for so little."

Of course, all this golf pleased Bing very much. He's always got his wooden shafts warmed up waiting for a hot pigeon to show. If he can't play, he's always practicing, as they found out at Claridge's, the very fashionable London hotel. At seven-thirty one morning the manager stumbled over Bing practicing chip shots in the hallway. The management suggested he replace his divot, pack his record machine, and get out. Standing out in the street, Bing explained somewhat indignantly to the newspapermen, "After all, it was raining, where'd they expect me to play?"

Henry Cotton told me that there are two hundred and seventy golf courses in Sussex County alone. Maybe that explains some of the long lunch hours and tea breaks that the English are so fond of. Of course, having so many golf courses so close together was ideal for me. With my slice I could enjoy three or four golf courses at the same time.

The British don't believe in golf carts. Their attitude is, "If you want to play polo, get a horse." I was used to riding a golf cart in America, so before walking eighteen holes I checked with a doctor. He said, "Don't worry about a thing, Mr. Hope. Play eighteen holes whenever you want."

"Thanks, Doctor," I said, "just for that I'll remember you in my will."

And he said, "In that case, play thirty-six."

Bing digs a very respectable divot, too. Between us, we

A script conference with our director. (United Artists photo)

moved more real estate than Bill Zeckendorf. We dug so many divots, Sussex is now in Devonshire.

The British are wonderful sportsmen. And so polite! Instead of hollering "Fore" when they drive a golf ball in your direction, they holler, "Awf'lly sorry, old chap, but you can get a new head under the health plan!" Maybe I've embroidered that a little, but you get the idea.

And of course, the British golfers we played were all very honest. They're all such gentlemen, they keep score accurately. They put down every stroke and never cheat. Naturally, Bing and I had no trouble beating them. Of course, when Bing and I played each other, it usually wound up in a deadlock. Actually, though, it's no fun playing with a guy who waits till your back is turned and then picks up his ball and throws it toward the hole, and who improves every lie. It got so bad for a while there, Bing refused to play with me.

Quite often, Bing and I would be out on the golf course when we should have been at the studio, working. The picture began to fall behind schedule. It's pretty hard to shoot a picture when the principals are not on the set. We've already had a picture with one Invisible Man; our crew was trying to film a picture with two Invisible Men.

After a while, our absence became noticeable. The director, Norman Panama, got tired of yelling, "Lights! Action! Where the hell are they?" He got into his automobile and drove out to the golf course looking for us. Luckily, we spotted Norm first, so we hid from him. But it wasn't easy. We played the last nine holes in a crouching position.

People ask Bing and me whether we ad-lib in the Road pictures. Actually, we like to embellish or as the writers say, foul it up. If you saw *Hong Kong* (and somebody must have seen it because I'm still working for United Artists) Bing and I had a scene in a harem where we are reclining on chaise longues with five or six beautiful handmaidens annointing us. I suggested that it might help my part of the scene if the camera went from a girl polishing my fingernails to another girl peeling grapes for me, down to a third girl painting my toenails. We did the scene three or four times and by the time we had a take, the toenails on my left foot were solid Surprise Pink. We finished shooting about five o'clock. I charged over to Wentworth Golf Course and played nine hysterical holes, rushed into the locker room to change shoes, sitting right across from two dour members. As I was discussing my game and what to do about it, I took off the golf sock from my left foot and these two members got a load of my Surprise Pink toenails. When

Road to Hong Kong. *I chased Joan Collins, Bing chased me, and the audience chased us. I remember Joan Collins but whatever happened to Pick and Pat? (United Artists photo)*

I raised my eyes to theirs, they gave me a look that's known as "Only his hairdresser knows for sure."

Now we come to the type of coincidence that can send a man to the electric chair. About two weeks later Bing and I were shooting a scene where we are returning from the moon and the entire populace is giving us the hero treatment—cheering, throwing confetti, etc. We did this scene five or six times until Bing got it right and for some reason or other most of the confetti was thrown at me.

We finished shooting at four-thirty and I dashed again for Wentworth. There I played nine frenzied holes trying to beat bogey and the dark. Once again I rushed into the shower, started undressing in front of two Scotsmen who had played thirty-six holes stopping only to eat a lunch they had packed. We were in the midst of a rather avid account of our golfing exploits when I took off my shorts and a load of confetti floated to the floor. They looked at each other, then stared at me—and I stood there looking like I hadn't taken a bath since New Year's Eve. From that day on the caddies at Wentworth always escorted me to the front tee.

Looking back, I realize that Bing and I overdid the golf bit. We played hooky a little too often. If Panama and Frank hadn't cracked down on us, the picture would have taken longer to make than *Cleopatra*. But, of course, not as much fun.

While we were in England, Bing and I also appeared on British television.

I appeared on a program called *Sunday Night at the Palladium,* one of the most popular shows in England, presided over by my old pal Val Parnell. For many years, Val Parnell was the boss of the London Palladium, their great vaudeville theatre. He loved American talent, and brought over the best. He brought to London such great American stars as Jack Benny, Danny Kaye, Jerry Lewis, Red Skelton, Judy Garland, Frankie Laine, and a great many others. During the war he brought over more Americans than Eisenhower.

CHAPTER THREE

I've always felt England was a great place for a comic to work. It's an island and the audience can't run very far.

The British people generally seem to disdain commercialism. (They've been brainwashed for years by the non-commercial BBC.) This attitude is mostly evident in the soft-sell on their commercial television. They do a lovely little domestic scene, and hidden somewhere in it is the product. They rarely refer to it directly.

The first time a product was mentioned on commercial television, three mice packed up and moved to the BBC. The big difference in those days was that in England the Government subsidized TV, in America we work on TV so we can subsidize the Government.

With nothing to do the first evening, I had an opportunity to sample some British television. They have a version of *This Is Your Life*, but the big emotional scenes aren't the same. When a little old lady met her son who'd left home thirty-seven years before, she merely looked up at him and said, "Alfie, your bloomin' tea's gettin' cold."

Some of the comedy shows are interesting, but because of local references and British vernacular, I found them hard to follow. I listened to one bit about a cricket fan yelling at the players, and all I was able to make out of it was, "Get up, Barret, you're not hurt—what a Nellie he is!"

The first time I appeared on British TV was quite an experience. I had expected to put in a few hours of rehearsal, but nobody phoned me or mentioned it. As it got closer to air time for the show and I still hadn't heard from anyone, I finally jumped in a cab and rushed to the studio.

I walked in, and the director said casually, "Oh, hello there. Nice to see you."

We sat down and chatted for a while. Finally I said, "When do we go on the air? When does the program start?"

He said, "Oh, we've already started. We've been on all along!"

How about that? I'd been blabbing away like a fool all that time, in front of twenty million people! For three weeks after that, I laid awake nights trying to figure out what I'd said!

I'd been to England before and this time I came prepared. I brought my own coffee. The British have a mental block about coffee. Either that or the word has a different meaning to them—maybe soup? Many words do have a different meaning in England than they do in America, and unawareness of this can often be embarrassing. One of my writers asked a salesgirl for soap chips and was told they didn't carry any. When he found them on the shelf, and before she explained that they are called soap flakes, he had her hysterical by remarking that she had given him a "bum steer." In England the word "bum" has quite another connotation.

Another interesting example of this "language barrier" occurred when we were about to shoot a sketch for one of my TV shows at the Wood Green Theatre. One of our crew, seated with the audience in the balcony, noticed that a door in the set had accidentally been left open by a stagehand. This would have spoiled the surprise entrance of Fernandel later in the scene. So he called to the stagehand, "Close that closet door," and much to our amazement this got one of the biggest laughs of the day, because what we mean by a closet, the British describe as a cupboard, while the word "closet" means toilet . . . not at all the sort of thing one shouts from the balcony. Of course, this was long before Jack Paar made a federal case of it.

In their own peculiar use of language, the British have as many surprises for us. Americans leaving an early morning call with the desk clerk invariably raise their eyebrows on learning that he will "knock them up at eight." And as long as I was there I never once dug the phone operator who upon placing a call for me would say, "Go ahead, you're through." I would always insist, "What do you mean through, I haven't even started." These little misunderstandings, I'm sure, were originally responsible for the Boston Tea Party. A recent re-evaluation of that little incident, however, has put the whole thing into more favorable focus. As one of our elder statesmen, Joey Bishop, has since remarked, "They shoulda kept the tea and thrown the town into the harbor."

When I was in London shooting *The Iron Petticoat* with Katharine Hepburn, I stayed at the Dorchester Hotel in the Oliver Messel suite—which could have changed the complexion of my fan mail.

You can get a picture of the Oliver Messel suite if I tell you that the plumbing is gold. Took me two days to get up enough moxie to use it. Messel is one of the finest of the English set designers, and he outdid himself in whipping up the background for my stay in the West End. I suppose the Messel suite was there long before I checked in, but it didn't really begin to play until I stepped into it. This lush setting, together with a small argument between two of my constant advisers, Charley Cooley and Monte Brice, prompted one of my writers to remark, "There's unrest in the Palace."

Before I get too far away from that plumbing, I'd like to mention one of the wonderful conveniences you find in most English bathrooms—heated towel racks. They simply expose from the wall a small section of the hot water pipes, thermostatically controlled, of course, so you don't back into a surprise. They say the English are a cold people, but believe me, in their bathrooms, they're the warmest.

The Oliver Messel suite was costing me seventy-five bucks a day and after the lavish press party the first day, I figured this was as good a time as any to move out. I reasoned that it was much too foggy to see any of the lovely view from the three exposures, that the noise of remodeling that was going on in that wing certainly didn't enhance it, and since I was working in the studio from early in the morning to late in the evening, there was about sixty dollars a day's worth of Oliver Messel I wasn't even using.

When he heard I wanted to move out, the manager, a charming limey named Greene, was terribly disturbed. He called me on the phone and said, "I must see you and talk to you." The accent fooled me. I thought it was Churchill, and told him to come up. We chatted amiably and had a drink together and when I told him I wanted to move, he said, "But you must stay here because—*this is you.*" Since then the suite has been occupied by Marlene Dietrich, Liberace, and Liz and Eddie. Sometimes now when I think of myself, I get a very confused image.

Ben Hecht's *Iron Petticoat* was made at Arthur Rank's Pinewood Studios. Pinewood is about thirty-five miles from the hotel and on the crooked winding streets, that's an experience. In London, if you travel in a straight line, they arrest you for drunken driving.

My chauffeur, Reginald Griffin, was an excellent driver and he was anxious to get me to the studio on time. On one turn, he pulled out and was in the process of passing a dozen cars when a truck loomed up coming the other way. Grif just managed to squeeze back into line in time to avoid a head-on collision, and for the next three miles one car hung onto our tail, blowing its horn all the way. Finally the driver pulled up alongside, and a dignified, but somewhat purple face leaned out and shouted to Grif, "You're

Katharine Hepburn trying to save a scene in The Iron Petticoat.
(*Courtesy of Metro-Goldwyn-Mayer, Inc.*)

a greedy 'og!" That's what I love about England—the whole
country is so well cast.

I'd never made a picture in England. In fact, it wasn't
until about six months before that I found out Paramount
wasn't my real mother. I was quite unprepared for what
awaited me.

The commissary at Pinewood, for example, is richly pan-
eled in oak with a thirty-foot high ceiling reminiscent of the
main dining salon on the *Mauritania,* and at times you have
the illusion that any minute you may be going down with
the screenplay.

The feeling of urgency, of fighting the clock and the
budget that one gets on an American movie set was nowhere

in evidence. Instead of yelling "Cut!" the director says, "Tea!" I wondered how these calm people would react in a crisis. It didn't take me long to find out. Early in the shooting of *Iron Petticoat* we had a fire on the set. No one panicked, they just seemed to regard the event with interest. After a respectful interval, someone remarked, "Look here—the set's on fire." A few of the grips on the catwalk converged on the blaze, a stagehand on the floor walked to a fire extinguisher, walked back to the flaming set, held the extinguisher aloft and inquired, "Would somebody care for this?" Then, as the stagehands were dousing and beating out the flames, the set decorator cautioned them, "Don't overdo it, children." I don't know, it must be glandular.

After the lush accommodations for actors in Hollywood, I was surprised at the extremes the British go to to save money. Instead of dressing rooms, everybody signs a "No Peeking Pledge." Which would have been fine with me, had I been in the wing with Diana Dors instead of James Robertson Justice.

But all the inconveniences are more than compensated for by one thing about an English studio that's entirely different from Hollywood. The technicians on the set treat you as an equal. And more than that, you get the feeling a picture is being made for the sake of Art, not money.

During one of the weekends on the *Iron Petticoat* schedule I had the opportunity to do a show at Dundee, Scotland. You may wonder why I would want to play a place called Dundee. Nearby at Carnoustie they have one of the world's finest golf courses. This very course was the scene of Ben Hogan's great victory in the British Open, and I wanted to take a shot at equaling Ben's great sub-par round of sixty-eight. I did—on the front nine.

I scored better at the show because I was lucky enough to get a really great audience. I told them how polite I thought British audiences were—they'd never think of throwing tomatoes . . . of course, it's just as hard to get

41

fish and chips out of your hair, I found out . . . I opened with an apology:

"I'm sorry I was late getting here, I was lost in the fog. I covered thirty miles before I found out I wasn't even in the car.

"I wanted to whistle for a cab, but I couldn't find my mouth.

"I wondered if anybody would find me out there and rescue me. Suddenly, I saw a light in the distance. Slowly it became clearer and clearer and finally I could make it out . . . It was the end of my cigarette."

They loved the fog jokes, especially since I impartially threw in a few California smog jokes. Everybody knows what California smog is—that's fog with the vitamins removed.

Actually, the fog in England is unbelievable. We were shooting at Pinewood one day when a fog warning came in and they closed down production at three in the afternoon so everyone could get home before it arrived. Not knowing what it was like, we dawdled a bit and when we stepped outside, we were amazed. It was so thick, we had to feel our way, which is pretty dull when you're traveling with Doc Shurr and Charley Cooley. Fortunately, our limousine was a Rolls-Royce equipped with wonderful fog lights. You just switch them on and you see the fog much better. We traveled for some time, supremely confident that our driver knew London like the back of his hand, when all at once it became apparent to us that he was following his knuckles.

I got out to investigate and found myself in a dead end street, and feeling along the walls of buildings, it appeared to be dead end at both ends. Then to my surprise, one of the ends which turned out to be a truck started moving and a long line of cars began to pass slowly. I would never have recognized which one was mine but for Doc Shurr hanging out the window peering into the fog with the aid

Hepburn and Hope in The Iron Petticoat. (*Courtesy of Metro-Goldwyn-Mayer, Inc.*)

of a cigarette lighter yelling, "Bob!—*Bob!*—Where are you?!"

But to get back to that wonderful audience at Dundee, I did a two-and-a-half hour show for them, throwing in every bit I could remember, and when I finished, they just wouldn't stop applauding. Finally I said, "What do you want?"

They said, "Do it over again."

If somebody ever comes up with a good process for it, there's an audience I'd like to have mounted.

One advantage in making a picture overseas is that it also presents a different locale for our TV shows. And while I was making *Petticoat* I had to turn out a couple of television shows for Chevrolet. I had a great opening joke about automobiles in England—"You know what a Rolls-Royce is—that's a Chevy that's been knighted," but somehow the advertising agency and I didn't see eye to eye on the humor of it. These people I worked for were rabidly pro-Chevrolet. The mere mention of another make of vehicle was enough to reverse the flow in their fluid drive. During the show we did in Alaska, we had a shot of a dog sled, and Dick Eastland, the account executive, wanted to put the Chevy insignia on it. I said, "Where do you put it, Dick, on the dog's nose? That's a husky not a Chevy."

At this time, I had a fairly full schedule—shooting at Pinewood, rehearsing for my television show, appearing on the BBC for various causes, and taping my daily radio show . . . For a while people started getting me on their electric razors.

Finding interesting guest stars for a TV program is no simple matter even at home, but here in London our problem was doubled. There are many talented English personalities, but unfortunately they were all in Hollywood.

We had already imported some fashion models from Paris, and the great French comedy star Fernandel was booked to appear, but we were still striving for something outstandingly unusual to present to our American audience.

The newspaper had mentioned that a Russian circus troupe was appearing in Brussels and we thought we'd make a try at securing the services of Popov, the wonderful Russian clown. Failing that, we might try filming some of the actual performance. It was a delicate mission and could, conceivably, be a little dangerous. Since it was my show, my problem, and my idea, I thought it only right that I should send somebody else. So I decided to send my producer, who also happens to be my brother, Jack.

Brother Jack had the traditional Hope enthusiasm for adventure and danger and before I was halfway through tell-

Jack Hope and distant brother. (Photo by Jerry Holscher)

ing him the idea, he had packed his bag, quit his job and booked passage home.

But by using a little brotherly persuasion and a photograph of the Unemployment Bureau at home, Jack finally saw it my way and agreed to make the trip to Brussels. The next couple of days were full of suspense. I left word with the operator to ring me any time of the day or night if Jack's phone call came through. I'd never forgive myself if anything happened to my brother or my plan. And not necessarily in that order. Finally, at two A.M. of the third day, Jack's phone call came through. Here's the phone conversation as near as I can remember it.

JACK: Hello, Bob?

ME: Jack! . . . What took you so long to call? We were worried about you.

JACK: Yeah . . . Well, we had a little problem here.

ME: Did you sign Popov?

JACK: The Russian secret police wouldn't even let me shake hands with him.

ME: Well, don't worry about it, they're all Communists. Just hop on a plane and come on back.

JACK: Well, I'll try.

ME: What do you mean, try?

JACK: (*Whispering*) Bob, there's a couple of Russian secret service men in the room with me now . . . They're a little stubborn about the film I shot of the circus.

ME: Where's the film now?

JACK: Lee's got it.

ME: Lee! You mean you took your wife with you?

JACK: I didn't want her to worry about me.

ME: I don't want to worry about you, either. Listen, Jack—you get Lee on the plane with that film right now, you hear?

JACK: Yeah . . . but what about me?

ME: You just stall them for a while . . . I'll get the Embassy on the—Hello, Jack! Jack! . . . Hello . . . Hello!

The line went dead and there was no way to get him back.

46

But Jack and his wife turned up safe and sound the next day, and I'd like to forget about that happy little incident . . . except if you hear of anybody who can use six thousand feet of a Russian circus, all on overexposed film, let me know.

They say that no man is bigger than his own shadow, but I must be the exception to the rule. My shadow is only five feet seven and his name is Louis Shurr. Louis, affectionately known as "Doctor," has been my motion picture representative since I tramped that first lucrative "Road" with Father Crosby.

"Doc" really believes in personal representation and as a result, he is rarely farther from me on my travels than a well-aimed rock. My trip to England was no exception and my suite at the Dorchester was separated from his only by the connecting door and a double-lock. On my side, I might add.

"The Doctor," friend, adviser, and confidant of many show business greats, ranging from Cole Porter to Sal Mineo, received his nickname for his uncanny ability to put his finger on precisely why a particular production is not coming up to expectations. When you're trying a play out of town, and Broadway is just a few performances away, and there's trouble with the second act (I don't know why, but it's always the second act), the cry goes out, "Send for the Doctor!" . . . Before you can say "Abe Burrows," Louie has leaped to New Haven, changed a costume, switched an act, deleted a song and dated the leading lady.

Another facet of the Doctor's engaging personality concerns his absolute fastidiousness regarding food. He believes that if you don't dine at Romanoff's, you're slumming. This brings to mind a memorable line uttered by Charlie Lee during the course of our flight to London. The stewardess had just served lunch, and the Doctor was poking listlessly at the food on his crowded tray, trying unsuccessfully to find a morsel he deemed edible. Charlie removed a lambchop bone from his mouth long enough to remark, "Doctor, you'd make a miserable prisoner of war."

It was principally through the devious Doctor's devices that we were able to secure the nine gorgeous French models who scored such a hit in the fashion parade portion on one of the TV shows we filmed in London. Armed with no more than his winning personality, his amazing business acumen, and a suitcase full of green stamps, the good Doctor was able to persuade the models to leave Paris and appear on our show. This friendly bevy of Gallic beauties almost caused the Doctor's undoing in his efforts to uphold his reputation as America's shortest Casanova. By the time he had dated Model Number Eight, he was ready for a rest cure.

The sequence with the nine Paris models from the House of Balmain, Lanvin, and Patou turned out to be no language barrier. I didn't talk to them onstage and they wouldn't talk to me offstage. Their routine proved to be very popular with the viewers . . . the women enjoyed the gowns, and the men appreciated what was in 'em.

That show also introduced luscious Diana Dors to American audiences for the first time . . . It wasn't until the following year that Miss Dors performed her celebrated Esther Williams impersonation by falling into her swimming pool clad in nothing more than an evening gown, two press photographers, and our own Doc Shurr. True to his craft as an agent, the Doctor, even while submerging, managed to keep ten per cent of himself showing. Miss Dors eventually dried out and went on to bigger and better publicity. Her appearance on our show proved her a competent performer, and one capable of garnering more than her share of laughs. A fact which may or may not be responsible for the delay in her return engagement.

The beautiful English singer Yana also debuted with us and it's a tribute to the great inner strength of the British that this gal is still up and around. Our show was being filmed at the Wood Green Theatre, a delightful draughty old barn that had been redecorated as recently as the reign of William the Conqueror. English winters being what they are, the meager heating facilities had to be complemented by the cast giving each other the hotfoot just to keep warm. Yana's number was scheduled to be filmed at 7:30 that evening, but what with tea breaks, and retakes, she didn't get before the camera until two A.M. Yana didn't finish her number "Young and Foolish" until five A.M., and that was just about the time "old and cold" was getting up for another day's shooting at Pinewood.

This was the year of the big freeze in London, and the severe winter was more than some tourists could stand. I was lucky, I had my California training. But having to make that early morning pilgrimage to Pinewood every day was getting tougher and tougher. I hated to leave that cozy central heating at the Dorchester for my studio dressing room, affectionately known as "Little America." I'd never have finished the picture if I hadn't bribed the studio doorman to come in and spray me twice a day with hot Bovril. The old water heater in my dressing room was working, but it was kind of tired. It gave off about as much warmth as an agent's handshake. I'm sure it was an old heater because it had a sign, *"For service, call Oliver Cromwell."* And that's living proof that old monologue jokes never die, they just turn up later in my reminiscences.

During a three-hour lull in my shooting schedule, I got a chance to see what some of the competition in the leading-man field was doing. I went to the premiere of *Richard III*, starring Laurence Olivier. I had a wonderful seat but had to change it when the Queen showed up. Her Majesty and Prince Philip arrived late. They were having the same trouble in those days—couldn't find a baby sitter.

The premiere was held at the Odeon which was appropriate because it's a very old theatre. In fact, Shakespeare is one of the ushers. At least I think it was Shakespeare.

Who else would say, "I pray you, sire—no smoking in the balcony."

The picture was wonderful and exciting, with three love affairs, five stabbings, and fourteen ax murders. If Shakespeare can keep it up, he'll be another Mickey Spillane. And it's amazing how realistic the battle scenes are in Vista-Vision. I retreated to the lobby three times.

In this connection, I think it's only fair to mention that British theatres have a bar in the lobby. They also sell candy, fruit, ice cream, and innumerable other foodstuffs during intermission. On this occasion, I think I had a Chinese dinner. It was nothing. Chinese food in England is all bean sprouts and onions and very little meat. The tip-off is they serve bread and butter with it. And it doesn't matter whether you're a party of two, three, or four, you still don't get the egg roll. Buddy Hackett would hate it there.

The reviews on our first TV show were barely cold before we started working on the second one. Incidentally, the show was very well received at home with the exception of a few suspicious reviewers who wondered how we were getting such big laughs from the Teabag Trade with jokes that were obviously aimed at American audiences. The fact is that ninety per cent of our audience was made up of American servicemen stationed in and around London.

We weren't too worried about our second TV show because we figured the experience we garnered the first time around would help us over the hurdles. Truer words were never spoken and I wish I had never spoken them. How did I know the British were going into the hurdle-raising business?

We had so many guest stars, my monologue was shorter than the Ten Commandments—and not nearly as sock. After all, I don't have Moses writing those one-liners for me.

The adagio team was scheduled to appear in a scene with the French singing star Liné Renaud. The scene was to take place in a French nightclub set, and Liné was to play the head of a nefarious syndicate who were being investigated by the Sûreté for smuggling California wine into France.

Don't stare at me—stare at my writers.

The scene opened with the adagio team doing their apache number—a wild, knockabout dance which included the traditional maiming and hair-pulling and reached its climax when the girl broke a prop-chair over the man's back. A nice, neat little tour de force with no problems. Only we didn't take into account the integrity of the British Prop Department. They built the breakaway chair so well, it didn't break. We could have called for a retake with a new chair, but where were we gonna get that dancer a new back?

But we can't blame the British for all our problems—the long arm of NBC censorship reached all the way over to England and Jack Paared us. Two of our guests, the Bernard Brothers, had been doing their act for thirty-five years without a breath of impropriety until a Blue-Pencil-Charlie from NBC's Honor Farm nailed them for indecent exposure. Their act is a hilarious take-off on different types of singers. They achieve a great effect by mouthing the lyrics of recordings played offstage and change costumes to suit the vocalists they're portraying. I thought they looked cuter than the Maguire Sisters in their wigs and dirndls, but NBC thought they had too much cleavage. We had to reshoot the whole scene with the Bernard Brothers wearing halters.

Another sequence we had in mind for the show never even got filmed. I had planned to invite the late Katie Johnson, a wonderful English character actress, to accept the "Best Performance by a Supporting Actress Award" on my show. She had won the award for her fine acting as the little old lady in Alec Guinness's memorable picture, *The Lady Killers*. She rejected my invitation, but I'll always treasure the polite note she sent. It said simply: *"Dear Mr. Hope:*

Thank you for your invitation, but I never leave my home in the winter-time."

Show business, anybody?

March and the rainy season were coming up fast, so we worked overtime to finish *The Iron Petticoat* before it had a chance to rust.

We had everything but the final scenes—in rough-cut, of course, and we gathered one wintry evening to see what Technicolor blessing we were about to turn loose on an unsuspecting world.

The lights went out, the picture came on and my entrance was greeted with appreciative cheers and whistles which lasted throughout the picture—I just couldn't restrain myself.

We had hopes of shooting the finish of the picture on an airfield in Moscow, but time and the State Department ran out on us. We finally did get an okay from the State Department, but that wasn't until three years and several chapters later.

We shot the finish on an English airfield made up to look Russian, and prayed the R.A.F. wouldn't misunderstand.

Then I packed my sterling silver salt and pepper shakers and any other odds and ends I thought the Dorchester wouldn't miss and reluctantly departed from the cold windy shores of Jolly Old. I loved being in England, and the wind never bothered me. Where else can you lay an egg and have it blow in front of another comedian?

CHAPTER FOUR

There's something going on back at the Pentagon that I don't understand. Every time somebody mentions my name, I end up with a snow job.

We've been to Alaska four times, Iceland twice, and Thule, Greenland, and the North Atlantic bases twice. I don't mind going back. It gives me a chance to visit my toes.

The first show that we ever did on film for television was back in 1954. Up until then TV had stuck quite close to the studio. The idea of going out to film in Thule, Greenland, where it's dark twenty-four hours a day, where the temperature is subzero, was frightening even to me. Fortunately we had a great gang of entertainers who helped make it all possible.

At that time, William Holden was a hot favorite in the Oscar derby for his superb performance as the conniving GI in *Stalag 17*. The Oscar he later won.

I phoned him and said, "Bill, how'd you like to help me do a show for the GIs up in Greenland over Christmas?"

There was a pause, then Holden said, "Bob, let me call you back in a few minutes and I'll let you know."

I said, "Okay, Bill," but as I hung up, I had the icy feeling that I was getting the Beverly Hills brush-off.

But ten minutes later, my phone rang. It was Holden. He said, "Bob, I'll go along on one condition."

I said, "What's that?"

He said, "That my wife can come, too."

Darn dogs—kept jumping in the sled with us. (NBC photo)

How about that? With Bill's beautiful wife Brenda Marshall coming along, I wound up with two stars instead of one!

I had heard a Pentagon bigwig was going to accompany us on the trip. I was delighted when it turned out to be a very good friend of mine, the late Secretary of Air Harold E. Talbott.

I tried to get Marilyn Monroe to go along on this tour. Marilyn wanted to go, but was prevented by studio commitments. We were faced with the problem of finding someone to replace Marilyn, which was next to impossible.

Bill Holden, Anita Ekberg, and dialogue director in Greenland.
(NBC photo)

I called several glamour gals, but for one reason or another, none of them could make the trip. I'd just about given up the search, when, a few nights before we were scheduled to leave for Greenland, I MC'd a Big Ten Conference Football banquet at the Biltmore Bowl in Los Angeles. Among the guests at the affair was a beauty contest winner, Miss University of California at Los Angeles. This girl was strikingly beautiful and, acting on impulse, I invited her to come along with us. Although she was virtually unknown at the time, this young beauty contest winner was to become one of our most glamorous stars. Her name? Anita Ekberg.

Anita is a standout, even in Hollywood where beautiful girls is one of the leading crops. To put it mildly, Anita is a spectacular by herself. On the tour I introduced her by saying, "Here's the greatest thing to come out of Sweden since smörgasbord!"

The GIs really went wild over her. Nature had certainly endowed her. When Anita walked on the stage, I'd say, "Her parents got the Nobel prize for architecture."

In addition to Bill Holden, his wife Brenda Marshall, and Anita Ekberg, we also corraled the fine comedian Bob Strauss, Hedda Hopper, Margaret Whiting, Patty Thomas, Professor Jerry Colonna, and actors Peter Leeds and Charles Cooley.

For music we had two bands, Les Brown's Orchestra and the United States Air Force Band from Bolling Air Force Base at Washington, D.C., under the direction of Master Sergeant John Osiecki.

We gave our main show in Thule on New Year's Eve. And let me tell you, Greenland is anything but green in the middle of winter. We landed in 36-below weather.

We were asked to remain in our seats in the plane, and after a short delay, we taxied into a heated hangar.

I said to Major Joseph Lynch, "This is extremely thoughtful of you, having us disembark in a nice warm hangar like this!"

He said, "Oh, we have to be careful, Bob. We don't want the plane to freeze up!"

It's nice to know you're wanted!

But that actually was the truth—in the arctic, everything freezes solid, and very fast. A jeep will freeze up in a few minutes. Some of the newer cars at the base had built-in heaters in the engine block. When you park your car, you plug it in like you would an electric toaster. Cars without heaters are left running the year around. The engines aren't even stopped for repairs, the mechanics work on them while they're running. We were told that one jeep at the base hadn't been shut off in six years.

Ever since I was a youth, I've been seeing cartoons about the nights at the North Pole being six months long. Well, now I can verify it. We were at Thule for three days and the sun never did show. It made me homesick for Los Angeles. Sunrise and sunset were about forty minutes apart, but it didn't really matter as there was no light to show for it.

It was dark when we arrived. We drove in pitch darkness from the landing strips to our billets, and then through the solid blackness to the building in which we were going to put on our show. It was eerie; it was like being on another planet. I can tell you right now, I'm not going to the moon until they get street lights! What a crazy country—where else can you get up in the morning and tune in the Late Late Show!

Along in spring, everybody gets out their sunglasses and waits for the sun to make its appearance. When it finally peeks over the horizon, a big cheer goes up and the rest of the day is spent celebrating.

After that, they get more and more sun till it becomes too much of a good thing. It really causes a lot of trouble. One guy opened a drive-in movie up there, and he went broke waiting for the sun to go down.

One GI said to me, "I feel silly coming home a little happy from a party at five in the morning, in broad daylight. You get the feeling the neighbors are really digging you!"

We put on our show in the gymnasium. If you wonder how a gym can be used as a theatre, let me say, it's very easy. All you need is the wonderful assistance of about two hundred GIs who work from morning till night erecting a temporary stage, laying cables, setting up lights and microphones, and filling the floor space with chairs. At every stop we've ever made, every show we ever put on, hundreds of servicemen put in a lot of hours of hard labor getting things ready for us. I can't thank all those guys enough!

We put on our New Year's Eve show in front of ten thousand men. I always start things off with a few jokes about the base and the surroundings. Here's a few I told the boys at Thule:

"I'm very happy to be here at Thule. The temperature is 36 below. We don't know below what, the thermometer just went over the hill! . . . It's really cold here. One guy jumped out of his bunk at 6 A.M. this morning, ran in and turned on the shower, and was stoned to death! . . . It was so cold last night, one GI fell out of bed and broke his pajamas! . . . Up here, a pin-up calendar isn't a luxury, it's a necessity! We certainly got a wonderful reception when we landed. All those soldiers standing at attention! I understand they've been that way for four months! . . . When I walked into General O'Donnell's quarters, the first thing I noticed was the tail of a reindeer sticking out of the wall over the fireplace. I said, "How come you didn't mount the antlers?" He said, "Don't be silly, it's not mounted, that's a live one trying to get warm!"

The weather isn't the only hardship the GIs have to put up with at Thule. Another gripe is the lack of female companionship. When we played Thule there were six thousand guys stationed there and only three women, nurses at the base hospital. Six thousand to three! You can have better odds than that at Las Vegas.

I said to one GI, "With no women, you must get pretty lonesome."

He said, "We sure do. When a wolf howls up here, it starts a community sing!"

On the stage, I threw in a few jokes about the woman shortage. I said, "It's so lonely here, one guy is going steady with his tattoo. And his friends keep asking him if she's got

"Off we go into the wild blue deep freeze." (*NBC photo*)

a sister! . . . You're not even allowed to think about girls up here. At night, a sergeant walks through the barracks and wakes up anybody with a smile on his face!"

The guys loved it. They roared at every line. After my monologue, we went into a sketch in which a couple of GIs write to the States for a mail-order bride. Anita Ekberg was the girl in the skit. When luscious Anita walked out on the stage, pandemonium broke loose. The men stood up and applauded and cheered and whistled as they feasted their eyes on this formidable Swedish beauty. The fact that she was wearing a very revealing gown that looked as though it were sprayed on didn't exactly act as a sedative on the excited GIs. Anita spoke her lines, but they couldn't be heard. The men were appreciating her other lines too much. Anita's 40-22-36 had stopped the show! We finally had Anita go back to her dressing room and change into something more restful. I mean, for the audience. I can't say that the change did much good. Anita is so richly endowed, she'd get whistles wearing a laundry bag.

All told I have more time on ice than a penguin in a Kool commercial. I made the Alaska scene several times during the war and several times since. I have two very vivid impressions of the Ice Box State: one is that they have great audiences and the other is that they have the most impossible flying conditions in the world.

We've had several close calls, one that's still playing reruns in my nightmares. We were on our way into Ladd Air Force Base in Fairbanks. The weather forecast wasn't great but five thousand men were waiting in a hangar down below to see our cast, Ginger Rogers, Mickey Mantle, Peggy King, and Jerry Colonna.

The field was socked in with what they call ice fog. After a long fight with the tower we got permission to come in on instruments. We fastened seat belts and prepared to let down. We were okay on cross wind leg and made the turn into final approach. Suddenly it was very quiet in the plane. There was nothing to see out the window, just black rushing past. We let down for what seemed like an hour. Then there was light below. We had overshot the runway. The pilot jammed on the power. There was a sickening lurch and then we had airspeed and started straight up. I don't know how low we came but after we passed over the officers club I found a drink in my hand.

We finally made it in at Eielson Air Force Base, a big B-36 roost. The ice fog cleared just long enough for us to touch the runway. By the time we were on the strip the field was closed in. We made it by bus back to Ladd Field

Mickey Mantle bats a thousand at Kodiak, Alaska. (NBC photo)

and while the cast chewed on some dry turkey sandwiches backstage Les Brown and the band were on the podium warming up the hangar.

We did a scene with Ginger Rogers in which she played "Klondike Lil" and I played the boob. I don't know how I always get the part. In the scene she was supposed to hit me over the head with a bottle. Naturally this was a breakaway bottle. It worked fine in Hollywood but it was a little colder in the hangar in Fairbanks. The bottle froze and when Ginger conked me I just stood there. I would have moved but I was unconscious. So she hit me again. That one woke me up and I hit the floor so fast Floyd Patterson would've been jealous.

Ginger quickly ad-libbed her way around until I came out of it. That's the joy of working with real pros. It's amazing how they can adapt themselves to any situation and work under any conditions. Ginger would rehearse all day, work two shows, and then visit the service clubs and dance all night with the GIs. And, believe me, very few of them were Fred Astaires.

The guys really flipped for Mickey Mantle. We did a sketch about the pampered modern army and used Mickey as a draftee dressed up in Doctor Denton's. The Mick enjoyed the whole bit and never goofed a line on stage. The guys all get a kick out of seeing the big athletes in person. I'm as big a sucker as they are.

I've had them all on the show at one time or another, Ben Hogan, Jimmy Demaret, Sam Snead, Doc Cary Middlecoff, Arnold Palmer, and Rafer Johnson. They all have that confidence that comes from being under pressure in public. And they all get big laughs which makes me wonder why they don't stay in their own business.

In 1959 we headed north to Alaska again. Steve McQueen, the handsome young star, was making his first tour with us along with his wife, the dancer-actress Neile Adams. Neile made a welcome addition and her singing and dancing turned out to be one of the highlights of the show. Incidentally, if you don't think Steve is quick on the draw, try saying "hello" to his wife.

Along with the wildlife and unexplored regions, another natural hazard in the person of Jayne Mansfield had signed on. Jayne has a talented eye for publicity and after the first couple of hours she found the trip dull because the motors kept going. When we landed at McChord Air Force Base in Tacoma to refuel, she slipped away from the troupe and

Hedda Hopper and Ginger Rogers go for a sleigh ride. What are the dogs doing in the back? (NBC photo)

Arnold Palmer and two pupils.

Here's Jayne asking me how to spell "Mansfield." (NBC photo by Gerald K. Smith)

wired ahead that she wanted to be greeted at the airport by a lion cub.

If you think you've ever had a test of your nonchalance, try shaking hands with the general and his staff while a lion cub is nibbling at your Paris garters. In spite of the panic, Jayne got the pictures she wanted and they were on the wire before the lion cub had buried my ankle bone.

There's never a dull moment with Mansfield up in the Yukon. If she bows, she could start an avalanche. On stage one day I asked the audience, "Would you like to hear

Jayne sing?" and a GI shouted, "I'd like to see her breathe." That kid should have been commissioned in the field.

It was late evening when we landed at Elmendorf Air Force Base at Anchorage, Alaska. The snowfall was pretty heavy. By the time our plane taxied in, we didn't need the landing platform. It was bitter cold, but I'll never forget those smiling faces on the boys as we got off the plane. They thought we were replacements.

At most bases a half dozen staff cars are put at our disposal, but there were none here. Just a few dog sleds which were very refreshing, to say nothing of quick freezing. Fortunately the hangar where our show was set up was only a few hundred yards away and we mushed the distance in record time. That is, all of us but Steve McQueen, whose hobby is racing sports cars, and Steve wanted to find out what this little dog team would do. What it would do, he found out, was fight with the dogs in the other sleds, so Steve decided to stick with the horsepower models.

Lieutenant General Frank A. Armstrong, Jr., was on hand to greet us and, in his capacity as Commander of the Alaskan Command, he made a short speech welcoming us. We've been friends since World War II, and I hoped I didn't strain our relations when I replied with a short ad-lib speech of my own. For openers I said, "It's hard to believe that since I was last up here this great territory has become a state of the union. Just think, all this slush is now Government property . . . Yessir, Alaska is officially a state—now they can send you here without a court-martial." Those GIs kept cheering right through Frances Langford's song.

We were assigned our usual quarters at the Château, a sort of French Provincial quonset hut. Actually, the rooms were very comfortable and we suffered no discomfort except for the heating problem. In order to keep everything from freezing, they were forced to keep the Château hotter than a New England boiled dinner. Outside it was below zero,

66

Sen. Stu Symington, Gen. F. Armstrong and an icebox salesman in Anchorage, Alaska. (NBC photo)

67

but inside it was family night at the Turkish bath. I opened the window once for some fresh air, took a deep breath and almost choked on an icicle.

The Château was our headquarters and we'd return to it after each excursion to the outlying bases. It was a great place to defrost and relax between shows. The food was excellent and the menu ranged from King Crab to Caribou Steak. King Crab, one of my favorite dishes, is a common delicacy in those parts, and it's served with alarming frequency. When I found some in my gelatin, I knew it was time to quit.

After doing a couple of shows a day, we usually spent our leisure hours in the lobby of the Château, and in typical actor fashion, the troupe would entertain each other. Tony Romano would strum his guitar, Colonna would unleash his trombone, Frances Langford would sing a couple of songs and Jayne Mansfield would burst forth with her specialty.

Ralph Evinrude, the motorboat engine tycoon, who is incidentally Frances Langford's husband, came along for the ride and wound up getting more laughs than anybody.

Good-natured Ralph was always ready to stab for the check at a party and naturally this boosted his popularity with the cast. But Ralph's biggest contribution to our entertainment at the time was his sleeping. Under ordinary circumstances, Ralph, by his own admission, was better than a raw hand at grabbing some shut-eye, but this particular night he was in fine fettle. He snored right through Colonna's air-raid siren impression, and darn near drowned him out. During this cacophony the waiter made his entrance carrying with him the tab for the evening's entertainment. Colonna grabbed for the check, but instead of paying it, he placed a pen in the slumbering Evinrude's hand, guided his fingers through the signature, and added a tip without Ralph ever losing a beat in his slumbering concert. We found out later that Jerry had signed his own name. To

Did Jayne need that chaperone? (NBC photo)

69

this day I've wondered if he did it out of pride or ignorance. "Evinrude" isn't an easy name to spell, you know.

With a couple of hours off, we did a little sight-seeing in Anchorage. Some of the characters walking the streets look like they're right out of Chaplin's *Gold Rush*—real tough looking grizzled grubstakers. Their only protection against the cold seems to be the bushy beards they sport.

The souvenir shops feature primitively carved desk sets and ornaments in ivory which are very expensive and don't look nearly so good as cheap plastic copies which can be bought back home. Fur, naturally enough, is a big item, and they've succeeded in working it into bow ties and lapel or blouse decorations which are supposed to be baby seals but look more like mice. Gives you quite a turn the first time you see one on somebody.

Fur coats, stoles, and parkas are in abundance but no cheaper than you'd pay for them at I. Magnin's or Neiman-Marcus because the skins have to be shipped south to be made up into garments and then shipped back to Alaska, and apparently no fur ever travels tourist.

Saloons and night clubs are plentiful in Anchorage and most feature servicemen's entertainment—booze and strippers. The men are aware they're mostly clip joints but it's the only game in town.

Some of the outlying bases we played had names right out of Jack London . . . Take King Salmon, a little upholstered ice-cube near Naknak. General Nick Nicrasson, head of the Air Force up there, flew over there with us to see how his own private Eskimos were doing. King Salmon is a radar base of great importance, and because of its complete isolation, the few hardy pioneers who work there are relieved at three-month intervals. This was the type of audience I reveled in, principally because I suspected I would be a welcome change from the dubious spectator-sport of walrus mating. There has since been some argument on this score.

I arrived at King Salmon wearing two parkas, sealskin

"Wishful thinking." (NBC photo)

gloves, and fleece-lined snowshoes . . . And if it wasn't for the mukluk I wore on my nose, my career would have been ruined. I mean it was cold. Up there it's considered spring when the temperature shoots up to 30 below. There's not much action for the men stationed there and naturally they become very weather conscious. They're always watching the thermometer. You really can't blame 'em, it's the only thing up there with a figure.

The landing field at King Salmon was carved out of ice and snow, and from our viewpoint as we approached it looked about the size of a dessert plate, and just as slippery.

We needn't have worried, though. Our competent pilot set our plane down in a deft skid that left us easily twenty feet from the side of a mountain.

Nobody walks around outside at King Salmon, everything's connected by tunnels. We emerged from one into a very large cafeteria, a mess hall big enough to accommodate over a thousand hungry servicemen. I might as well admit that I try to eat *before* a performance because some of those mess sergeants can get awfully nasty after watching my act. This particular mess sergeant had really knocked himself out trying to please us . . . The main course was a roast suckling pig. Or rather, a facsimile of a roast suckling pig, because the artistic chef had doctored an enormous ham so that it resembled a porker's head, complete with an apple stuffed in its mouth . . . I wonder if he was trying to tell me something?

After lunch we gave our show inside a hangar from which the planes had recently been removed. Enough gas fumes remained to forbid smoking, and it was required that prospective smokers do their inhaling outside in the 35-below weather. During the show I could tell from the color of the faces exactly how much of my audience I was keeping interested. If you're interested in the score, rest assured that I rivaled Picasso during his Blue Period. Here's a sample of what might have sent them for their cigarette break.

"Well, here I am in Alaska. (*Sneer.*) So much for your Early-Warning System!

"But I'm happy to be here with you ladies and gentlemen of King Salmon, walruses, seals, and caribou. It's a state now and everybody's got equal rights.

"Alaska now has the only senator who wasn't seated—he was mounted.

"I was anxious to get here. I saw the Air Force recruiting poster for King Salmon. Golf, water-skiing, outdoor barbecues . . . I thought they were kidding . . . until I saw a second lieutenant on the spit outside."

A lesson in underacting. (*NBC photo*)

One of the scenes we decided to do was perfect for the guys in these lonely outposts. It was called, "Operation Egg Roll," and it concerned two Japanese soldiers on a deserted two-by-four island in the South Pacific who didn't know the war was over. I played the Japanese GI, and Steve McQueen was the chicken lieutenant who was still drilling me fifteen years after the Peace Treaty. He had me marching so much, we wore out the island. And although there were only two of us, he still insisted on a separate officer's mess. When he learned the war was over and Japan had lost, he decided the only honorable way out was for us to commit hari-kari —but this time he wanted the enlisted man to go first.

The scene was a fine cross section of GI gripes and voiced the popular notion that the only real enemy in any war is the officers. Our audience ate it up. I kind of got a bang out of it myself. Japanese is one of the real fun dialects to do, and not too difficult if you just bear in mind that they are a nation of ventriloquists. You never separate your teeth, and speak with practically no jaw motion. In order to avoid suffocation, you have to suck in air between your teeth, which fortunately for most Japanese is no problem at all. For me it was a major engineering feat and once or twice I thought I'd inhaled my caps. But it's the only way to acquire that lovely hissing sound . . . the one coming from the stage, not the audience.

I'll never forget the guys up at King Salmon. There are four hundred men manning this installation in the middle of nowhere. There isn't a settlement for hundreds of miles. Most of the buildings are connected with long corridors so the men rarely have to go out into the bitter below-zero cold, but it's a molelike existence with the quality of a recurring nightmare. We were only there for a few hours and in that short time the long corridors began to take on an unreal perspective.

Three hours and fifteen minutes later we were off the stage and on our way back to Elmendorf and Christmas dinner.

Captured USO soldier.

The flight from King Salmon was very festive. Everybody was in a mellow mood. Coming into Elmendorf Field, I was up in the cockpit talking on the radio to the tower, trading a few jokes. I asked the tower man, "When are you going to clear us for landing—we're late for Christmas dinner." He replied, "You can land as soon as we get this big fat red-face guy with the reindeer out of the flight pattern."

Christmas Eve at Elmendorf had that certain old-fashioned greeting-card quality . . . The tall pines with their branches heavy with snow . . . the white mountains almost blinding you with their brilliance . . . the heavy imprints where a wandering moose had crossed . . . Only the deep ruts left by a jet bomber kept the scene from looking like one of Grandma Moses' specials.

"Twelve O'clock High" General Armstrong and his staff hosted our Christmas Eve party, and it was a ball. At each place setting were tiny silver cigarette lighters with our names and the symbol of the Alaskan Command inscribed on them. Everybody had seen our act by now and we had to come up with something a little different. We did some special lyrics to my old standby "Thanks for the Memory" and incorporated the names of all the officers and men who had made us so welcome. Squeezing in a handle like "Lieutenant General Frank A. Armstrong, Jr., Commander-in-Chief of the Alaskan Command" would have used up the whole lyric, so we didn't use it. I wonder if he'd ever been called "Butch" before? Everybody came up with something unexpected. Jayne Mansfield sang "White Christmas." And in that dress, it certainly was.

I was so impressed with Jayne's singing that a couple of years later when the Defense Department dared us to visit Thule again, I invited Jayne to go along. She was thrilled with the idea of going to Greenland, or as she put it, "It sounds wonderful, Bob, I've never been to South America before."

Along with our usual group we were lucky enough to get

The twenty-four-hour alert crew lends an enthusiastic ear at Harmon Air Force Base in Newfoundland. (NBC photo by Gerald K. Smith)

Dorothy Provine, of "The Roaring Twenties," and Anita Bryant, the beautiful young recording star. Anita brought along her husband, Bob Green, a handsome young man with a lot of ugly muscles. And as the frosting on the cake, we also signed Miss World, Rosemarie Frankland. As a matter of fact with this cast they didn't need me. I just went along to carry the bags.

That fellow in the Defense Department with the sense of humor mapped out a beautiful tour of resorts for us. Argentia, a soggy naval base on the tip of Newfoundland; Harmon Air Force Base, a vital SAC link, also in Newfie; Goose Bay, a nice little ice plant on the over-populated shores of Labrador; and of course my two home towns, Sondrestrom and Thule, Greenland, where it's always dark and it's just as well.

Then just so the big cities wouldn't spoil us they added the Riviera of the North Atlantic, a base called Frobisher on Baffin Island. Frobisher is so far out that it costs a dollar to send a post card. It has a population of five and that's counting caribou and ice worms.

I asked our pilot where Frobisher was on the map and he said, "Oh, it's not on the map."

"Well, how do we get in there?"

"With that weather, by boat. It's the only SAC base in the world that uses kayaks."

But we did get in and it was a beautiful crystal-clear day, one of the three clear days that year. We played in a tiny gymnasium to an audience of American Air Force, Canadian Air Force, Canadian Royal Navy and Mounted Police. Jayne did it again and right in front of the audience. She looked out at the Mounted Police in their bright red dress blouses and said, "I didn't know they were real, I thought they just had them in the funny papers." I hope Nelson Eddy never reads this.

The weather didn't get to us until we hit Thule. The morning was clear and quite warm, somewhere below zero. I don't know exactly what the temperature was because the thermometer went over the hill.

Secretary of Air Eugene Zuckert and I bundled up and went out to officially open an ice road between the base and a nearby Danish village. I later found out that the road had been officially opened three times that week.

The afternoon show went fine, but just as we were finishing a voice came over the P.A. system and announced that a "Phase One" had been declared. That meant that winds

Secretary of Air Eugene Zuckert and I attend a pajama party in downtown Greenland. (NBC photo by Gerald K. Smith)

up to forty miles an hour had suddenly come up. In Thule that's just a balmy breeze. By the time we left the gymnasium a "Phase Two" had been declared. That's a windup to sixty miles an hour. It didn't sound like anything when I heard the announcement, but when I stepped outside the door, I missed my car by sixty feet. It was impossible to move alone, you had to lock arms with three or four people and feel your way through the blinding snow and darkness.

Within thirty minutes, all roads were blocked with cars

that had been abandoned in drifts. We barely made it back to our quarters, where we sat sweating out the weather.

They announced that a "Phase Three" was expected. That's the ultimate, winds over a hundred miles an hour, everyone confined to their quarters, emergency rations, and sandbags piled around the general.

Then came the call from the commanding general that I didn't want. The evening show would be canceled. I begged him to hold off for a while. An hour later, the wind was still howling, but the buildings weren't leaning quite as much. I told the general that if it was at all possible the cast wanted to do the show. He said, "Wonderful, Bob, but I can't guarantee you much of an audience on a night like this."

I've always been an optimist, and with good reason. We played that night to a house that was jam packed. There was standing room only on the rafters.

I stretched out in my bunk that night exhausted but feeling good. We'd wrapped up another trip and without a mishap. Then the phone rang.

It was Jayne, and she was hysterical. And believe me with Jayne, that's a lot of hysteria. When I finally got her simmered down, I found out that she had lost an earring. "Jayne," I said, "look around the floor. On second thought have Mickey do it, I know it's difficult for you to look down."

"Bob, you don't understand. I lost it out in the snow."

"Jayne, go back to bed. It's pitch dark outside, it's twenty below zero and there's a gale blowing. No man in his right mind is going out there to search fifty thousand acres of snow for a diamond earring."

A few minutes later, I noticed some lights going past my window. I looked out and there they were. At least a thousand GIs with flashlights searching for Jayne's diamond. Never underestimate the power of a woman.

Oh, incidentally, Jayne did find the earring. She had two of them on her right ear.

CHAPTER FIVE

There's a very apt saying in show business: "If you don't go over budget in Paris, you're either very rich or very sick."

You don't have to worry about me on either count. I made a picture in Paris and went one million dollars over budget.

I refer to a little epic I made for United Artists called *Paris Holiday*, or as it was known in the trade *Around the Bank of America in Eighty Days*. We were so far over budget, we had to develop the negative at Rexall. Of course, you run into special problems in Paris. I was there three weeks before I remembered I went there to make a picture.

As it turned out, I was just showing Hollywood the way. Since then Darryl Zanuck spent more on *The Longest Day* than it cost to shoot the real World War II. Marlon Brando wouldn't come out of his dressing room until *Mutiny on the Bounty* was ten million over. And by the time the asp had gotten to Liz Taylor in *Cleopatra,* the studio had lost more than Eddie Fisher.

As a result, they made Darryl head of the studio, Liz and Marlon are more in demand than ever, and, as I write this, I am on my way to Africa to made my fourth picture for United Artists.

And how does it all start? With a simple phone call. That's one of the things that knocks me out in this racket. You pick up the phone and the next thing you know you're winging off to Africa for a picture, or over to Korea to play an Army camp, or out to Glendale to christen a driving range. It doesn't matter what. It's a new place, new people, new sights. Suddenly you're up, you're stretching forward instead of leaning back.

I had just got back from the Far East junket when I got a call from Bob Benjamin, Arthur Krim, and Max Youngstein, the big moguls at United Artists. They heard that I was free from Paramount and wanted me to make a picture for them. That's the kind of call that does it for me—a nice message for the ego and a little help for the bank account. And from three of the most intelligent and astute gentlemen in the business. I say this because they really are, and not just because they liked an idea I had for a movie.

Actually, it wasn't a story idea, it was more of a mood, I could see a big ocean liner leaving on a trip, like the *Queen Mary* or the S.S. *United States*. I could hear myself doing the narration over it. I was going to start it out as close to real life as possible. I would be an entertainer on his way to Europe in search of a script. That's all . . . just a man in search of a script and the complications that evolve.

That may not sound like much of a story, but look what Hemingway did with an old man, a rowboat, and two worms.

The boat idea really appealed to me. Back on Broadway I had once appeared in a musical called *Say When*. There was a shipboard scene and I had gotten some pretty big laughs. Comedians are like elephants—I mean aside from Jackie Gleason—they never forget a laugh.

That was it, we would start on a ship. Now where was the ship to go? I had just finished a picture in England, so London was out. What about Rome? We could never top what's going on there now. Paris? Ring-a-ding-ding!

Paris, bewitching, fascinating, exotic, deductible Paris. The melting pot of the world, something's always cooking. Where *l'amour* is the national anthem. The whole country's one big drive-in movie. Paris, the place where the wife is

Martha Hyer and two of the Ritz Brothers. (United Artists photo)

referred to as the other woman. The only city in the world where My Sin outsells Coco-Cola.

A couple of days later I had lunch with Max in New York and he bought the idea. And that's how *Paris Holiday* was born. We shook hands on the deal and I decided against dessert. If I was going to be my loveliest in front of the camera, I'd better start shaving a little off the pot. And just by way of polite conversation I asked, "Who'll we get to produce it?"

"You," he said.

"Me?"

"You," he said again. And he hadn't been drinking. I ordered dessert. I was going to need my strength. Producer! Maybe it would work. Maybe it might even help. Many times a producer and an actor don't see eye to eye . . . Sometimes it's impossible from the position the actor is in.

As soon as I got to Hollywood I called Ed Beloin who had written many pictures for me, including *Favorite Spy, Road to Rio,* and *Lemon Drop Kid.* We kicked the idea around, developing new bits, new angles, new places for the plot to go. When we had it whipped, he teamed up with Dean Risener and started on the back-breaking task of turning out a shooting script in twenty-eight days.

Then came the problem of casting the girls—my kind of problem.

For the glamorous spy we got Anita Ekberg. I'm the kind that likes a lot for his money and that's Anita. After Thule, Greenland, I knew what kind of an effect she had on an audience. And she's wonderful to work with, even though she's not too good when you have to go out on location. It takes her an hour to pack and that's before she gets to the luggage.

I was a little nervous when we signed up Martha Hyer. She is an exquisite fragile beauty and she is young. That much I could forgive. But on top of all that she is a talented actress. I just hoped there would be enough Oscars to go around.

When I thought of Paris, naturally I thought of "Horsehead," the great French comic Fernandel. A year before he had done a television show for us in England. The results were *fantastique.*

Getting Fernandel to appear on that TV show was one of the few times that my agent, Doc Shurr, had to call upon me for assistance. He returned from Paris with the news that

Pulling away from Ekberg. Some of my better acting.

Fernandel wouldn't consider making an appearance for less than forty thousand dollars.

Fernandel was a great admirer of mine, the Doctor related, and he regretted that I hadn't come to discuss the matter with him personally. That was all I needed. A few hours later I was in Paris shaking hands with Fernandel.

Through an interpreter, of course, he convinced me that because of his great admiration for me he would appear on my television show for nothing. Naturally I kept refusing his generous offer just long enough to make certain he wasn't kidding. Then I accepted.

His only stipulation was that I furnish transportation to London and expenses for himself and his family. Any guilt I might have had about Ferny's "free" appearance soon vanished. The tab I was presented with after Ferny and family departed (leaving an empty wine cellar at the Dorchester and a corps of exhausted waiters in their wake) almost equalled the salary he demanded in the first place.

I knew then why he and his family had insisted on traveling by boat train—they were too heavy to fly.

The interesting part of our first meeting was that though neither of us understood a word of the other, we were somehow able to communicate through some sort of an international language of comedians. While I was explaining to the interpreter in English what the point of a joke was, Fernandel had already dug it from my facial expression and was supplying the appropriate reaction. I was able to do much the same thing during his French explanations.

Ferny told us jokes in French that none of us understood but were able to laugh at just from the expressiveness he displayed and the timing. Actors at Lindy's react the same way. They understand the language, they just don't listen to it. They wait only for the pause that indicates the end of the punch-line and launch into a story of their own. It's the basis of a joke about a group of comedians and one of them tells of losing his job, his money in the market, and his wife and child in an accident, and when he pauses for sympathy, another comic says, "That's very funny, did you hear the one about—"

Ferny would be perfect for the picture. We sent a wire to Paris in the ridiculous hope that he might be available. He was open from April first to June first. A little too close for comfort, but a little too late to worry about it. We started contract negotiations.

Marquee-wise we seemed pretty well set. There was Fer-

Trying to get my salary back from Fernandel. The Horsehead and the Hustler. (Photo by Gérard Décaux)

nandel and myself for those of you who dig comedy, and Anita and Martha for you deep thinkers.

Inasmuch as I was acting in the picture and producing it, I was tempted to direct it. However, wisdom prevailed over ego. If anything went wrong, I would need someone to blame. Gerd Oswald was our man.

I had worked with Gerd many times before, at Paramount, when he was an assistant director. He was a real driver, one of the best in the business. He had done a lot of television shooting in Europe, and had just directed a feature-length picture in North Africa.

Gerd was to take care of the pre-production setup. There was little time left. He packed his beautiful wife and flew to Paris.

I finished the last of my television shows and booked passage on the S.S. *United States* for the following week. Meanwhile Martin Gang phoned with disturbing news: Ferny would not sign his contract without reading the script. If there's one thing I hate it's actors who think.

Beloin and Risener raced over to the house with a final draft of the script. I blithely put it in an envelope and airmailed it to Ferny. Then, with the clear conscience of a monk and the optimism of a used-car buyer, I left for New York and a leisurely crossing to Paris. I would arrive there on Sunday and the picture would roll on Monday.

The second day out from New York I was bent over the rail. It wasn't the ocean, it was the news from Paris. I wasn't present but as nearly as I can re-create what happened, it topped anything Greta Carbo did in *Camille*.

Ferny's agent, Teddy Wimpress, had received the script and rushed over with it to his client's apartment. Ferny was delighted. He grabbed the envelope and dropped in an easy chair. He smiled in anticipation.

Now, of course, Ferny could not read English and had no idea of the plot or the dialogue. So he did what any actor would do. He could make out my name "Bob" and he could make out his name "Ferny." He started counting the speeches. On the first five pages there were a lot more "Bobs" than there were "Fernys."

This was only the first five pages. He was philosophic. He spat on his agent and went on. Next came three more pages and there were no "Fernys" at all. The mascara really hit the fan.

Fernandel called in the French press and issued a statement: He was betrayed by the American comic, Mistaire

Hope. He had been promised a co-starring role but instead he had no part at all. The script was bad. I was bad. America was bad. American chewing gum was a fraud. He would not do the picture. The deal was off. *Sacre bleu!*

Fernandel grabbed three bottles of wine and disappeared into his bedroom. The story was front page all over Europe. It was picked up by the wire services and headlined in America.

It was a big afternoon for the overseas operators. The telephone in my cabin never stopped. Smadga, the United Artists representative, radio-phoned from London. Gerd called from Paris. Both of my attorneys were on the horn, Norman Tyre from Paris and Martin Gang from Hollywood. It was very nervous outside.

I arrived on the boat train from Le Havre and checked in at my favorite towel warehouse, the George Cinq Hotel. This hospitable little mint was bulging with tourists. There were so many Americans in the lobby, they should have a sign on the desk: "French Spoken Here."

Rooms were at a premium, but Monsieur Blue, the manager, was kind enough to give me his penthouse suite. He had to, I don't think he could afford it.

As I entered the living room, there was a rather small welcoming committee, just Norman Tyre thumbing through a catalogue.

"*Bon soir*, Norman," I shouted gaily and somewhat Gallicly.

There was no answer.

Figuring my French was a little too Montmartre for him, I tried a simple, "Hi, Norm."

Still no reply.

"Norman, it's me . . . the fellow that signs the retainer checks. What are you doing?"

He looked up impatiently. "I'm looking for a replacement for Fernandel." He continued thumbing the French casting directory.

"Norman, if we don't have Fernandel, we don't have a picture. Now stop worrying and let's have a drink."

He rose to his feet and said, "If we don't have a picture, we can't afford a drink." He walked toward the door. "Oh, by the way, welcome to Paris." He closed the door on my face.

I made a mental note to appoint him morale officer.

Shortly thereafter, Mort Lachman and Bill Larkin, my writers with luggage, arrived from Hollywood. I had sent them a rush wire from the boat. They hadn't had time to pack any clothes but it wasn't going to make much difference. How formal do you have to be when you're chained in a hotel room?

We had dinner and talked over the script. We were meeting with Ferny's group in the morning and wanted to get a few peace moves planned. Then, bidding them a pleasant first night in Paris, I had the house detective show them to their room and lock them in. I got into my pajamas, checked under the bed wistfully, and stretched out.

I'm not what's known as a troubled sleeper. When my gourd hits the pillow, it's Nytalsville. It would take a fire alarm to wake me up. That sounded at four A.M.

There was a pounding at the door. I opened it and was greeted by a cloud of smoke and a disheveled assistant manager. He shouted, *"Feu! Feu!"*

"This is no time for baby talk," I yelled. "What's happening?"

Looking down at my barbecued toes, I realized that *feu* was French for fire. I grabbed my American Express checks, my porcelain caps, my make-up mirror, covered my head with a wet towel and rushed out into the hall.

There was a panicky mob in the corridor. Always a cool one in emergencies, I quickly trampled over the women and children and made my way down the stairs to the lobby and out into the street.

For an emotional race, the French certainly have calm

firemen. They just sat in front of the hotel in their shiny red trucks, wearing their shiny chrome helmets, and waited while the chief went inside to inquire if there was anything he might do.

As it turned out, the fire was confined to one residential apartment. A crepe suzette had backfired. That's the French for you—food you can read your newspaper by. The blaze had a good first act but the second act was going downhill. I wandered across the street to an after-hours brandy-and-egg bistro called the Calvados.

And so at five A.M. I had my first breakfast in Paris, one brandy neat. It's got orange juice beat a mile. The room was a crush of happy people. The French are such a light-hearted people, always gay and laughing. Of course, you'd be gay and laughing, too, if you started your day with wine on your Wheaties. Yes, they really know how to live, wine, women, and wine. They're the only ones I know who go home for a coffee break.

The feeling was contagious. Suddenly the world was brighter and there was still four hours until the meeting with Fernandel.

The meeting was set for ten A.M. in my suite. It started out like an emergency session of the Security Council. My battalion arrived first: Mort and Bill, Norman Tyre (still carrying the casting directory), my agent Louie Shurr (dressed in black for the occasion), and my aide-de-camp Monte Brice.

Next came the money men, or as they are affectionately known, the Soreheads, Smadja and DiMarco from United Artists. They took chairs in the center of the room, the neutral camp.

Fernandel's entrance was carefully planned. He was preceded by two lawyers and his agent, Teddy Wimpress, a sign of pessimism. He was followed by two writers, his brother-in-law Jean Manse, and playwright Serge Verbere. This was more optimistic.

Fernandel paused at the doorway, then rushed across the room, threw his arms around me, and covered my cheeks with Burgundy kisses. He pumped my hand.

Agents turned to agents, lawyers stared at lawyers, they were incredulous. From the wild shower of French it appeared that Fernandel was glad to see me.

He was. What had happened to the blood feud? Well, you have to know a little about Fernandel, and for that matter *all* actors, to understand.

Ferny started out as a kid singing in the dives of Marseille. It's a tough port town and you have to fight to make it at all. He went from there to the clubs of Paris, to the stage, and now he is an international hit in pictures. He had to scuffle for every extra song, for every spotlight, for every line, for every scene.

It's the same for everyone. If you've got star billing, you've battled for it.

Ferny could top the best of them. I wish you could have seen him as we all went through the script together for the first time. He would look until he found a page or a scene without his name on it. Then he would carry the script around the room, by that page, groaning, moaning and beating his breast. We got his message.

At five o'clock that night, we were still at it. We had stopped only to feed and wine Ferny. He went through fifteen dollars' worth of room service before he put his napkin on.

We reached an agreement. Ferny would do the picture if we would rewrite it, building up his part. The picture would not start into production until the script was complete.

Now that same day we had officially taken over our space at the Studios Boulogne. In addition, we had our film crew on call, cameramen, electricians, grips, set designers, and so on ad extremely nauseum. While they were idle, they were on full salary. Our cast was standing by at full expense.

We worked frantically. Every day between ten and five

the meeting with Fernandel and full committee took place in my suite. From five at night to five in the morning, Mort and Bill worked with me on the changes. Our suite was a shambles. We had interpreters, for every line of script had to be done in two languages. We had typists, messengers, chauffeurs, and even a mimeograph machine which we had to smuggle into the hotel.

The daily meetings with Ferny were extremely difficult, mostly because of the language barrier. I only speak a little pigeon French. Just enough to get by with the little French pigeons. Until I went to Paris, I don't think I really believed people actually spoke French. I thought it was a bit that Maurice Chevalier had borrowed from Hildegarde. As for Fernandel, his English was limited to "Talk to my lawyer" and "Wheech way is the bank?" Not a very imposing vocabulary, but one designed to keep the bouillabaisse pouring in.

When you're sitting around talking jokes and situations, it's tough enough in English, but to have it translated, that's impossible. What would normally have taken ten minutes to discuss would take an hour. The frustration of not being able to speak directly to someone is almost unbearable. And when the others are jabbering in their language, you are torn with curiosity and suspicion.

In our language our conference would have taken two days. It was ten days before Fernandel shook hands over the script and we were ready to roll. The delay cost us two hundred thousand dollars.

Actually it was more than that, thirty-six hundred dollars more. Before he left, Fernandel cornered me and informed me that although he had an apartment in Paris, his legal residence was Marseille. He would need thirty dollars a day extra expenses, technically he would be on location. I know a master's touch. I agreed and gave him my watch, my ring, and my belt buckle to seal the deal.

CHAPTER SIX

The day I start a picture I feel good. I even look better, possibly because I have make-up on. At last the business is through and you are permitted the illusion that you're an artiste . . . until the first rushes come back.

I was due at the studio at noon. That's the schedule they work in France, from noon until seven o'clock. Anybody on the streets in the morning is assumed to be on his way home.

Monte phoned from the lobby to tell me that Jacques was waiting with the car. Jacques was to be our chauffeur for the next four months. After my first ride with him, I doubted that any of us would make it.

The French law says a driver must yield to the right . . . and that's the only way they yield. It is considered unsporting to even look ahead, or behind, or to the left. One half of the windshield is totally wasted. The French drive like Paris is still occupied by the Germans. And Jacques is typically French.

He didn't get a regular salary; he was paid by the accident. As we screeched through the cobblestoned streets, I tapped Jacques on the shoulder and said, "What's the matter? Are we lost? We just passed Notre-Dame Cathedral for the third time!"

And he yelled back, "The way I drive, m'sieur, I thought you might want to pray."

Studio Boulogne is about ten kilometers from the hotel. With anybody but Jacques it would be a magnificent drive. What a beautiful city . . . the Champs Elysées with its cafés and beautiful women, the Rue St.-Honoré with its smart shops and beautiful women . . . the Bois with its lake and beautiful women. That's what I like about Paris . . . it's built!

The studio wasn't anything that Desi would want to buy. Your contract there is strictly a real estate deal. You rent the bare walls and then bring in everything else, cameras, lights, sets, even typewriters, files, and chairs. The actual sound stages are small, and lined with straw for sound purposes.

However, what may be missing in physical facilities is certainly made up for by the crew. The French love motion pictures. They take a great pride in their industry and in their individual crafts. The crews are young and extremely ambitious. Today we are seeing the results: their "baby" directors are now running in the money at the box office.

When Gerd yelled "Silence . . . *Moteur*" and the cameras turned for the first time, we were already deep in the financial hole. The delay had cost us two hundred thousand; Ferny's expense money thirty-six hundred more.

Contrary to what certain comedians have led you to believe, the national French pastime is picnicking. To go on a picnic, you must have a holiday, and each holiday cost us about ten thousand dollars. Let's take May. There was the Worker's Holiday, Armistice Day, Joan of Arc's Birthday, and Mr. Hulot's Holiday. Altogether we lost twelve days, one hundred and twenty-thousand dollars. Believe me, that's a shoebox full of francs.

If you can't lose a whole day, there are always ways to lose a half. Each principal in the picture is assigned a dresser or valet. He sees that your wardrobe is in condition, that you are wearing the right costumes for the right scene. How could a dresser cost you five grand? Easy. Mine wore my shirt out for the evening and didn't have it back at the studio in time. What about my duplicate shirt? He left a hot iron on that one. I still think he was sore because he wasn't assigned to Anita.

Did you ever have some snapshots come back scratched? You lose eighty-five cents and you change drugstores. In our racket it runs a little higher.

We were shooting a big interior set, the main dining *salon* of the S.S. *Liberté*. All the principals were involved, me and Ferny and Anita and Martha plus twelve featured players and three hundred extras.

We'd been going at it all afternoon. When you work with that many people, the going is slow. Finally, on the seventh take we knocked it. We were all delighted till our head cameraman, Roger Hubert, called a halt. The negative was scratched.

This is panic time at a studio. Was the camera at fault? Was the film at fault? How much of what we shot was spoiled?

Here it isn't money that worries you, the negative insurance takes care of that. But the delay was a problem. Ferny had commitments. We only had the studio for a limited time.

The fault was in the film. The laboratory in England discovered that one technician had passed the film over eight rollers instead of nine. It cost the insurance company twenty-five thousand dollars. We had to reshoot the whole sequence. It cost us two and a half precious days.

A few years ago when that would happen at Paramount, Bing and I would smile at each other and say "Pity." We'd grab our golf bags and disappear until the posse came after us.

Now all these problems were mine.

After days like this at the studio and the nerve-shredding ride back to the hotel with Jacques, it was about all I could do to make it to the room, have dinner sent up and fall in the pad. What a waste! There are so many great things to do and places to see in Paris, the Rue de la Paix, the Arc de Triomphe, the Bastille, all wonderful restaurants, and on the Diner's Club, too.

One night as I was racked out on my pad, spooning a little gruel, the phone rang. It was Dean Martin. "Bob, this is an emergency. I gotta see you right away."

I didn't have to ask where he was. I went downstairs and directly to the bar. Dean was in Paris to make *The Young Lions* with Marlon Brando and Montgomery Clift.

He was seated alone. I crossed to his table and would have shaken his hand but he had a glass in both of them. I welcomed him to Paris and then asked, "Well, what's the emergency?"

Dean said, "I've been with Brando and Clift for two weeks. Sit down. I just wanna spend a few minutes with somebody I can understand."

We dined that night at one of the finest restaurants in Paris, La Crémaillère. You know the type, it's the kind of restaurant where dinner is twenty-five dollars a plate and you have to catch your own snails.

After the brandy, as I sat there casually ignoring the check, Dean spotted a beautiful blonde. French women are among the most attractive in the world, and they're very popular. Especially with men. But this girl was stunning. She looked almost like Marilyn Monroe and wore her hair exactly the same way. She got up to go wherever girls go. As she passed our table, she winked at me. Dean hurried me out into the cool night air.

That weekend Ferny had a dinner party for the cast at the Chez Vincent. I was seated next to Anita when the same beautiful French blonde joined our table. Ferny introduced us, "Bob-bee, these ees Cochcinelle."

I bowed gallantly. "I almost had the pleasure the other evening at La Crémaillère." I kissed her hand.

Cochcinelle smiled knowingly. I turned to Anita. "Beautiful, isn't she?"

"Yes. Isn't it a shame," she said.

"What do you mean, a 'shame'? It's great."

Only his hairdresser knows for sure. Cochcinelle on the set of Paris Holiday. It's a simple story—"Boy meets boy."

"Bob, don't you know? Cochcinelle is a female impersonator."

"You're pulling my leg!"

"I might," Anita said, "but Cochcinelle never will."

I felt like a farm boy on his first visit to the big city. Cochcinelle is one of the big nightclub stars of Paris, does a strip act like you now see in Las Vegas. She, or I should say It, has a figure that rivals Anita's and it's just as real. Yet, and this is a weird one, Cochcinelle could pass the physical at the YMCA. I wish I could have another talk with my father.

In mid-May we moved out of the studio for our first location shot. We rented a château in the little village of Gambais about eighty kilometers from Paris. It was a new challenge for Jacques, he got three chickens the first day, just missed a farmer who was a little too nimble for him.

The château was beautiful, real picture-book style, 34 rooms, all unheated. The lack of heat was hardly a concern, after all, this was practically summer.

For the first time in the history of France, it snowed in May.

Every day for a week the cast and crew huddled in front of the fireplace. As the temperature dropped, we would break up odd tables and chairs and sneak them into the fire. By the time we left the château, there was standing room only.

The snow job cost us five days' shooting. A word of advice from a producer with a frost-bitten wallet: take out snow insurance. I don't care if it's July. I don't care if you're shooting in Ethiopia. Buy snow insurance.

Then there are those normal calamities that can happen to anybody:

Because of the clouded skies, we needed lights inside and outside. There was no power available, so we rented gasoline generators. Then we found out that gas was rationed and

Norman Tyre spent three days down at City Hall. We spent three days in the dark. If it wasn't for Ferny's teeth, we wouldn't have had any light at all.

One of the featured actors who was to play the part of an insane man actually did go mad.

When we went to reshoot a matching scene with a custom red convertible, the car was missing. It had been loaned to a couple who left for a honeymoon in Holland.

We may have had trouble getting the movie going, but our kitchen never stopped. In most countries when you're on location you're required to feed the cast and crew their noon meal. In America, that's no problem. You knock 'em a peanut butter sandwich and a dipper of Hawaiian punch and that's it. If anybody complains, they're up before the House Un-American Activities Committee.

In France it's a little different. Lunch isn't a meal, it's a production number. We had to serve a seven-course meal. By the time lunch was over, everybody'd forgotten the plot. We had one cameraman and seven cooks.

We served three kinds of wine with every meal. We were pouring it faster than they could stomp it. The service yard was a sea of empties. It looked like homecoming week at Mogen David.

Every spring there is a big benefit for the French war orphans. This year, Ingrid Bergman headed the program and she asked me if I would perform. For a cause like that I could hardly refuse.

Eddie Constantine, the young American who went to France and became one of their leading picture stars, offered to translate for me.

Without rehearsal, I was limited to a monologue and picked what seemed a natural topic: making a picture in France.

There was a tremendous audience that night and they were extremely receptive. I would say the line in English.

Eddie would repeat it in French and get the laugh. The timing is kind of odd, but it didn't bother the audience. Eddie got some huge roars on lines like these:

"It's very frustrating making a picture in Paris. We work hard all day at the studio to get a love scene just right. Then, on my way home, I see couples on every street corner doing it better.

"The French are much more broadminded than we are. I told Fernandel the plot of *Lolita* was about a middle-aged man who makes love to a twelve-year old and he said, 'A twelve-year old what?'

"Our progress on the picture has been slow. We were held up three days on production. Somebody lost the corkscrew.

"At present we're three weeks behind on film and six weeks ahead on wine.

"Now I know what they mean in France when they say labor is high.

"But it's a wonderful way to live, and not a bad way to go, either. The average Frenchman is still smiling three months after he's dead."

The reviews in the Paris newspapers were excellent. One of them printed my picture and quoted all the jokes. I could hardly wait to get to Gambais that morning to take a few bows.

There was no crew to bow to. They had been called out by their union. They felt my jokes degraded the French workman.

I met with the union leaders and apologized. I explained that these were jokes (I often have to explain this). I told them that we did the same jokes at home about all the workers, including the President. The next day the walkout was withdrawn.

If there was one thing in the picture the critics really liked it was the chase scene where I dangled from a helicopter. A man dangling from a helicopter over Paris! We weren't in enough trouble on the ground, we had to take to the air.

I hate to disillusion you. I did not actually hang from the plane, but a stunt man did. He hung from a copter while it soared in space, dipped over buildings, flew him through signboards, through trees, and narrowly missed buildings.

Before you can fly a helicopter around Paris at low altitudes, you have to get a permit from the police. Unfortunately, the police were not feeling too kindly toward American film companies at the moment.

The late Mike Todd had been there shooting *Around the World in Eighty Days* and wanted the streets cleared for one scene. Without asking anybody, he had hired tow trucks and had all the cars pulled away. Parisians were still screaming.

We hired Captain John Crewdson to handle the stunt flying. He brought over three helicopters from England. The planes alone cost two hundred dollars an hour. The first day the planes were ready, the crew was ready and the stunt man was missing. We thought he had turned chicken. We discovered he was driving a motorcycle in a race at Nice.

The script called for the helicopter to fly over the River Seine with me dangling from a rope ladder. Just as I passed over a barge, the whistle was supposed to blast and hit me with steam.

We had to find a barge with a stack. There was no such animal. So we rented a plain barge and put a stack and whistle on it. The next morning the camera crews were briefed, the planes were sent aloft, and the stunt man dangled from the copter high over the river. The pilot zeroed in on the barge. It was a big zero. There was no barge. C'est la loot! The barge captain had gotten a better offer. He was up the river and we were up the creek.

Three days later Captain Crewdson had to return to England. He left a young able pilot in charge. I hope his leg is healed.

As Wrong Way was taking off with the camera copter, he brushed a tree and broke the rear rotor. The plane spun crazily and crashed to the earth. The pilot broke his leg, the cameraman and his assistant were miraculously safe, but I'm afraid the Technirama camera will never work again.

There was no problem here, we wired to London for another one. They wired back: REGRET TO INFORM YOU ALL AVAILABLE TECHNIRAMA EQUIPMENT TIED UP ON VIKING PICTURE IN COPENHAGEN. IMPERATIVE YOU RETURN ONE OF YOURS. URGENT.

We did the best we could. We dug up the pieces and sent them back in a shopping bag.

Probably the most chic affair in Paris was the Gala at l'Opéra. A "gala" is any big theatrical affair, usually what we would call a premiere. This one was for the opening of Otto Preminger's *Saint Joan*. Fernandel and I were asked to entertain and, inasmuch as this was also a United Artists' picture, we were anxious to cooperate.

I really didn't need an excuse. My ego could never turn down a chance to appear on the stage of the famous Opéra. There was a full symphony orchestra playing the overture. Les Guards Républicains lined the grand staircase in their musical comedy uniforms.

The stalls were spilling over with jewels and furs. Celebrities were a franc a dozen. The President of France was there. So was the Mayor, Salvador Dali, Yul Brynner, Deborah Kerr, Michele Morgan, Gerard Philipe, Eddie Constantine, Jean Seeberg, Ingrid Bergman, Charles Boyer, Eva Gabor and, of course, Anita and Martha.

I was extremely nervous and I had a right to be. A top-hat crowd is the toughest audience in the world. Ferny and I had worked out a pretty good gimmick. He would introduce me in English and I would introduce him in French.

Our entrance was fine. He spoke in English and got yells. I spoke in French and there wasn't a sound.

It was my first formal bomb. Luckily I was wearing a stiff shirt, it was all that was holding me up. We did a sketch, a tourist and a French waiter. The idiot cards wouldn't fit in the prompter's box and they had to hold them up one word at a time.

We were working in French, but I wasn't worried. I had learned my cues phonetically. All I had to do was hear them. I didn't. Ferny had forgotten his lines and was ad-libbing all over the place. I was standing there with soufflé on my face.

I never did see *Saint Joan*. As soon as the lights went down, I split for the hotel.

I figured I'd hide in my room until it all blew over. The next day the reviews came out and we were a smash. As a matter of fact, we were treated better than the picture. I still wasn't happy.

I asked our dialogue director, Louise Vincent, what had happened. "How come Ferny got screams when he spoke English and I got stoned when I spoke French?"

"But Bob," explained Louise, "Fernandel is one of us. When he speaks English badly it is ludicrous. We laugh. You are a guest in our country. When you speak our language, we are proud. If we laughed, we would be insulting you."

Her story was a little skinny, but I bought it. Life was brighter, the world was round again.

Our twelve weeks' shooting schedule had elapsed. A new picture had taken over our space at Boulogne, we had to move our entire setup across town to Joinville.

It was now June. Instead of snow we were fighting a ter-rific heat wave. Add to this a hundred and fifty arc lamps burning and no air conditioning. One day the gas from the arc lamps sent sixty people to the dispensary.

One scene for the chase had me running after a ladder. It took us twelve takes to get it. In the heat my make-up kept sliding off. Anita had her problems, too. She had a scene in which she wore a fur coat. And that's all she wore, a fur coat. It didn't seem to bother her, but the rest of the crew was a wreck.

Johnny Rapp and Les White must have a lot of talent. These two writers are still working for me, even though they came up with the idea for the carnival scene. I was worried about the cost, but Les looked at me with those big pussy-cat eyes and said, "It'll be the cheapest thing in the picture. Don't build anything. Find a little carnival and shoot the scene on their day off." Johnny chimed in, "You can use the carny owner as an extra. He'll probably pay *you.*"

The carny operator didn't pay us. We had to pay him. We didn't rent his carnival. We had to buy it. That guy got enough out of us to keep him in cotton candy for the rest of his life.

When we assembled the carnival, it occupied almost a full city block. It took every floodlight in Paris, London, and Amsterdam to light it.

Then we hit a power snag. When we turned on our lights, the city of Joinville went dark. The mayor was pretty upset, as were all the mothers who were changing diapers at the time.

We had to agree not to start shooting the scene until midnight. That meant "golden time," double salary for the entire crew. Instead of a thousand dollars an hour, it cost us two thousand dollars.

I was on time. Martha was fifteen minutes late. Horsehead was an hour late. It took another thirty minutes for him to put on his make-up and comb his mane.

At two o'clock we were finally ready to shoot. The scene was lit, Ferny was preening in front of the camera, resplendent in a gray-striped suit, the best boy was standing by with clapstick. Suddenly Olga Gow, our eagle-eyed production assistant, turned to me and asked, "Wasn't M'sieur Fernandel wearing a checked suit in the last scene?"

I don't have to tell you the answer. Ferny was sent back to change. The checked suit was not in his dressing room. It had been left at Studio Boulogne some forty kilometers the other side of town.

While I sweated out the next hour, I rode on the Ferris wheel. At least I only had that sinking feeling half the time.

At four A.M. we were again ready to roll. Ferny was in his checked suit, Martha was in her lavender gown, and I was in a sweat.

Gerd yelled, "*Moteur!*" and the scene was going great when Anita walked in with her husband Anthony Steele. She took one look at Martha and yelled, "But lavender is my color!"

The argument alone cost $2000.

The last scene of the picture shows the four of us in a car in a big triumphant victory parade down the Champs Elysées. If you look closely, you'll see that the parade goes one way and the car goes another.

That's the way it was with the budget and the money. Somewhere between the first scene and the last scene we had gone a million dollars over.

But it was worth it. The picture had everything: murder, intrigue, suspense, mystery, horror, romance, VistaVision, Technicolor, and stereophonic sound. In fact, for a while there we didn't think we were going to need any actors.

I'd do it all over again just to see Anita walking down the streets of Paris. What a sight! It was the first time in French history the Eiffel Tower looked like the Leaning Tower of Pisa.

And what a privilege to work with Fernandel. I've kidded him a lot but he's one of the most talented comedians I've ever shared a screen with. If he ever learns to speak English, I'll personally see to it that he never gets past Ellis Island.

We found out what a lot of studios have since found out: You can't save money by going to Europe to shoot. But you meet some great people, you work with some fine crews, and the scenery looks great in color.

As I look back there's only one thing that still puzzles me. If France gave us the Statue of Liberty as a present, how come it turned up in our production costs?

CHAPTER SEVEN

In the fall of 1957 I had my annual cheery call from the Air Force telling me that the Christmas tour this year was to be routed to the Far East. It was seven years since I'd entertained in Japan and I figured they'd had time to heal. Also, I needed a bath again.

I don't know how the word gets around—maybe my phone is tapped—but before I had a chance to mention it to anybody on my staff, everybody was packed and waiting at Burbank.

Our take-off was delayed an hour and a half. The weather was fine, but somebody forgot the club soda. Finally, we were sealed in to what would be our little home away from home for two weeks, and got clearance from the tower. We seemed to be a long time going down the runway and suddenly it occurred to me, "They forgot to weigh Hedda Hopper's hats." But luckily Jayne Mansfield's costumes made up for it and we took off.

A lot of people like to look out the window on take-off. I'm afraid to. I usually find Jerry Colonna looking in. Somehow he'd made it on time this trip, and there he was on the seat beside me, curled up in his mustache.

Up forward, the cabin was alive with activity. Barney McNulty had my idiot cards spread all over the floor, printing the jokes I'd never have time to memorize. Barney didn't get off the floor for twelve days, which is quite an accomplishment for a guy who doesn't touch the stuff.

McNulty is another of the growing group of vagabonds who have become infected with the Hope brand of wander-

Hollywood columnist Mike Connolly, an unidentified coolie, and the fortune cookie is Jayne Mansfield. (NBC photo)

lust. I might add that Barney is the king of the idiot card business. He moved in during the early hectic days of television when actors had the enormous task of memorizing whole new scripts weekly. Barney can copy a complete scene on big boards with three-inch lettering faster than I can read it. On our show this is particularly important. We work right up until I walk out on stage making last-minute changes, a new line, a new bit, if something is big in the news, a whole new monologue subject. Many times I am telling the first jokes while Barney is printing the last one. Fortunately he does not break under stress. In fact, Barney is often responsible for relieving tension with little jokes.

Like the time I was driving on the freeway shortly after an item had appeared in the papers that my trip to Moscow was finally authorized. I had no doubt about McNulty's willingness to go along, for passing me at that moment was Barney's station wagon and as he went by, he held up an idiot card that said, "Have red ink—will travel."

Once he held up a card, chastising a lane-changer who was cutting in and out, with the provocative question, "Would you like to try for a new car?" The other driver lost his sense of humor long enough to ram Barney's rear end.

After that, Barney confined his idiot card jokes to the studio. On one show I came out to perform a dance number with James Garner. Neither one of us could exactly qualify for An Evening with Fred Astaire, so naturally we goofed the routine two or three times and had to stop the cameras for retakes. On the fourth take, what really broke us up was Barney holding up an idiot card with an Arthur Murray type dance lesson showing the position of the feet.

The cue card man must remain anonymous, do his job silently and confidentially so that the actor stands up and looks like he is picking the words out of the air and thereby create the illusion to the studio audience that it is extemporaneous. Barney has mastered this knack and is the king of his racket.

If possible, he works any show that I do a guest appearance on. I learned this the hard way. One day a few seasons ago I was guesting on the Roy Rogers show. I was only doing a monologue, so I skipped the rehearsal, rushed in from the golf course, patted my cheeks, straightened my eyebrows, walked out in front of the audience and started into my monologue.

There was a new idiot card man. After each joke he took the card and threw it over his shoulder into the audience. It's tough enough getting laughs in this business, but when you have an audience hiding under their seats to keep from getting speared by the corner of an idiot card, you've really got a problem on your hands.

It wasn't until the middle of the monologue that the producer dug this action, grabbed the Card Man and banished him to CBS. By this time as far as getting laughs there was no chance. Right about that time I bought a hundred acres in the San Fernando Valley and started to raise a few more Barney McNultys.

Some comics don't need idiot cards. Sid Caesar gets along without them, although he probably has the jokes tattooed on his eyeballs. As for me, if I ever arrive at the Pearly Gate, and Saint Peter starts asking questions, I just hope Barney is there with the idiot cards.

But to get back to the Far Eastern trip . . . the writers were at their machines, polishing some of the pearls they'd prepared for me; the cast was gathered around me rehearsing; and Les Brown was busily at work on an arrangement. He was arranging his hand for a bridge game that lasted fourteen days. I've always envied musicians—nothing upsets their way of life. Les has a bass player who came out of a PX carrying only a bucket when everyone else was loaded down with exotic souvenirs. I wondered what he wanted with this ordinary bucket till we all showed up at the plane hot and sticky to find he'd filled the bucket with ice cubes. "Buckets" as he has come to be known, cooled it the rest of the trip.

Approaching Hawaii, we were treated to a rare sight—the sun low in the Pacific, hanging effortlessly in a cloud-free sky over the bluest of blue waters, and Mickey Hargitay giving Jayne a pedicure. I know Jayne has sexy toes, but to be uninhibited enough to kneel in the aisle, reveling in Revlon, before the jaundiced eyes of one's fellow workers requires a degree of savoir faire of which very few males are capable. I couldn't help but admire the superb detachment of this Cuticura da Vinci.

There may also be a few sour grapes clinging to that last paragraph, for one thing I learned on this and other trips —Mansfield is a great trouper. She never complained about anything, and there were times when she had loads of provocation. Before each stop we made she had to change into a new costume, and in the tiny lavatories on the plane that can be a chore . . . particularly with Mickey in there to help her. Man, now I know what they mean by togetherness.

The military made our arrival in Hawaii a very memorable affair. Lined up at the foot of the ramp were a platoon of the prettiest WAVES in the Pacific. As each member of our troupe came off the plane, he was greeted with a friendly smooch and a lei thrown about his neck. I had leis piled up so high, I couldn't get my hat on—although after that reception it wouldn't have fit me anyhow.

Lined up on the other side of the ramp were half a hundred of the local brass. The troupe introduced themselves to the first officer in line who relayed the introduction to the man at his left and so on. If you didn't have a memorable name, what with the band blasting away, it suffered somewhat in the translation, and fellows who started out at the top of the line as Peter Leeds, for example, wound up at the end as Herman Goldfarb.

Pete, who deserves better identification than that, is a fine all-around actor, who loves to travel. I can always tell Christmas is approaching when a face with big sad eyes in it pops up in the unlikeliest places and asks, "When are we leaving?"

He came out of a sand trap on the fifth at Lakeside last year. The year before, he turned up in my bathroom. I opened a jar of Bufferin and there he was. I've carried the Bufferin with me ever since.

We were four hours late getting into Hickam Field, and our audience of sixty-six hundred at Bloch Arena had been sitting in their seats those four hours for fear of losing them. That's how starved they were for shows. With that kind of enthusiasm, we skipped dinner—an audience like that is solid caviar.

Les Brown and the boys had rushed over as soon as the plane touched down to warm up this audience and I think most of his cats were playing without instruments—although with Les's band it's hard to tell. Anyway, if I've ever seen an audience that didn't need warming up, this was it.

Not to put too fine an edge on their appetite, I brought Jayne Mansfield out almost immediately and a roar went up that had me looking over my shoulder for the lions—I knew who the Christians were.

I reminded the boys that Jayne was wearing a special dress for the occasion—made of two hundred yards of barbed wire. I don't know why that line goes so big. Maybe it reminds the boys of the stockade. When she stepped out on the stage, so many flash bulbs went off, I thought the Japs were playing a return engagement. For five solid minutes they popped away with their Brownies while I stood there regretting not buying any Eastman Kodak stock. This audience included a group of British Army engineers who'd flown all the way from Christmas Island just to see the show, and when Jayne made her entrance, I got the distinct impression that they were digging a tunnel toward the stage. I quickly went into a routine with Jayne, and when she walked off, enough of the audience followed her for me to get the message. From there on in she closed the show.

It was close to midnight when we finished at Bloch Arena and were whisked to Don the Beachcomber's for a late snack. On the way, we drove past Henry Kaiser's village which is kind of a rabbit's-eye view of the future—everything is pink—but beautiful and lush looking. And to think he put the whole thing together starting with nothing but money. They've got a swimming pool at the village that has a sliding cover which serves as a dance floor. All it needs is somebody that's on the juice to push the wrong button and you've got a real Hollywood party.

Kaiser has really done a tremendous job at his Waikiki playground. When he bought the property for two and a half million, there wasn't even any beach with it—just a rugged coastline of coral rubble. So Hank made his own beach, dragging in three thousand truckloads of sand. That's almost as much as Bing sprays out of the traps at Thunderbird. Then he put up two hotels fourteen stories high and rented the rooms out as they were going up. If you slept late, you had a good chance of being cemented into the foundation. One guest called room service, but they refused to bring his dinner up to 1202 because the hotel was only built up to the ninth floor. They told him to come down to the dining room and watch that first step.

Don the Beachcomber is a great host but he's rum-happy, and after an hour of his flowing hospitality you're grateful for the native floor show and the gentle breeze from the grass skirts among other things.

Thirty pineapples later, or about three-thirty in the morning, we were wheeled back to our stratocruisers for the take-off to Wake Island. One big advantage of the stratocruiser on these long hops is that while the rest of the troupe curls up for the night with their sleeping pills in reclining seats,

Honolulu—actor learning to shoot back. (Photo by Signal Corps U. S. Army)

there is a little room in the deck below that can be converted with a luxurious litter to a bedroom for the star.

I had just stretched out on this canvas heaven when I became aware of something moving on the floor beside me. In a moment my eyes became accustomed to the darkness and I recognized Leo Monsky, feature writer for the Hearst papers, who was covering the trip. I helped him to his feet and asked if he was all right, although I could see he wasn't. We got him up on the litter and the crew brought some

S. Pacific. Paying off my "Claque." (Copyright © 1944. Paramount Pictures, Inc.)

oxygen which helped a little. We sat up with Leo for the rest of the night. We didn't learn until later when they examined him at Tokyo General Hospital that he had had a mild heart attack. But it takes more than a heart attack to stop most newspapermen, and Leo stayed right with us covering the whole trip.

A few hours before Wake we crossed the international date line and the crew had a little ceremony for people making it for the first time. After you're blindfolded they explain that anybody crossing the date line has to be

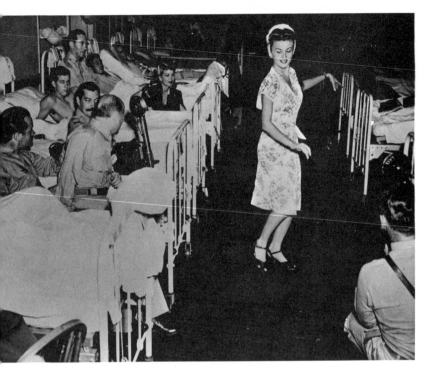

Patty Thomas making a few patients happy in the S. Pacific. (Copyright © 1944. Paramount Pictures, Inc.)

dunked into the Pacific. You go along with the kidding as they help you into a Mae West, and tell you not to worry, the plane's altitude is only fifty feet now and a destroyer has been assigned to pick you up. But you can't help worrying a little when they lead you down the aisle and you hear the back door opened up and feel the rush of wind about you. You have no way of knowing they've only opened the door to the rear luggage compartment, and what you're standing on is only a suitcase, and some sort of ridiculous bravado prompts you to jump when they tell you to. I wanna tell you the six inches back to the floor is the longest trip I've ever taken. Mansfield was lucky. With a Mae West on they couldn't get her through the doorway.

Honolulu to Wake Island is a long hop and by now we were all unconsciously looking at our watches. This was little help since some of us were still on Los Angeles time, some on Hawaiian time, and some on Wake time, which is a few hours earlier but a day later.

Wake is a little grain of sand in the vast Pacific and you wonder how those bus drivers up front manage to stumble over it, but somehow they always seem to. At any rate, I was making some such remark to Jerry Colonna seated beside me when he reassured me with, "Don't tell me, tell Amelia Earhart."

The official population of Wake is 875, including only 70 women. I thought there were seventy-one gals, but the one I counted on never showed up.

There's a lot of history in that tiny island, only slightly larger than the Hollywood Bowl's parking lot, and several grim reminders of its finest hour still remain. The bombed-out airfield huts are mute testimony to the bravery of Major James Devereux and a handful of Marines who held out against the Jap hordes for sixteen days. And off the southwest coast, its rusted hull projecting from the surf, is the *Suwa Maru*, torpedoed by a U.S. submarine.

You'd have to see it to believe it, but Wake Island actually has a golf course, or if you like, a golf course has Wake Island. I was gonna play a round when I arrived, but the tide was in. They use the course for fishing at high tide.

Jayne Mansfield shook up the barracuda when she went for a dip in a pink angora bikini studded with rhinestones and pearls. That was the day most of the male population took up skin-diving.

The rest of us fought the heat under some warm salt-water showers. This wouldn't have been worth mentioning except for the fact that the Wake Island laundry had broken down a couple of days previously and towels were nonexistent. The cast used the honor system (at least one eye closed) as we took turns romping around under the tropical sun in an effort to get dry.

Laundry continued to be a problem on this jaunt because getting at our luggage in the plane's hold would mean the loss of too many hours in loading and unloading. The Wake Island PX had its meager stores depleted by our gang who were willing to settle for anything in the way of clean shirts and sox. Colonna, in a tucked-in mumu, looked like a displaced mau-mau, and I wound up in a dickey-fronted tuxedo shirt that would have played very large at a Polish wedding. Les Brown's band handled the laundry problem with their usual aplomb—they ignored it. Frank Cleaver, an NBC executive, who accompanied us on the tour, still wears his purple heart proudly. It was awarded to him for being aboard the band's plane the day the air conditioning quit.

This was the third day of Operation Box Lunch, and we were understandably weary of ham and cheese sandwiches, olives and pickles—especially for breakfast. Just the thought of the nice hot lunch awaiting us at the Wake Island mess hall after the show was enough for me to polish my drool cup. The lunch was everything I thought it would be—tasty, succulent, and savory . . . Unfortunately our plane was refueled and ready to go . . . so we ate it on board, en route to Okinawa—out of boxes.

Kadena Air Base on Okinawa is just three hundred miles from Red China but we lived like filthy capitalists, sleeping in real beds for the first time in three nights. The Air Force billeted us in very lush VIP quarters that only cost us a dollar a night, and if that doesn't lick Communism, nothing will. On top of that, the Okinawan girls working as domestics each day launder any linens you leave on the floor, press any clothes left on the bed, and shine any shoes left outside

ELEVATION 10 FT.

The Bermuda of the Pacific ▼ The Land of the Big Winds

Another *big wind arrives in Okinawa.* (*NBC photo*)

the door. We were asked not to spoil them by overtipping more than a few cents a day. Spoil 'em? We wanted to stow them away and take them home—you never saw such beautiful service.

Our first night on Okinawa we rehearsed till the small hours of the morning a spy sketch we would be doing for the boys. This sketch had a large cast which we recruited from the ranks of the reporters covering the trip, and right here and now I want to say that Mike Connolly, the *Hollywood Reporter* columnist, only looks like a butler who is supposed to be a Chinese spy, getting him to perform like one is a whole career. And Irv Kupcinet plays every scene like a man going into business for himself. But without the newspaper people doubling as actors the scene would have been just me and Jayne Mansfield, which is actually the way I prefer it, but somehow in these decisions I always seem to constitute a minority of one.

Early next morning our troupe left by bus for White Beach where we were to do a show on the heavy cruiser U.S.S. *Los Angeles* tied up in Buckner Bay. White Beach is now just a small army pier, but in World War II it was the site of the Marines' gallant landing. I was enjoying a few extra winks when I was aroused by the gentle roar of a helicopter which seemed to be coming into my bedroom. Instead it landed on the lawn outside—my personal limousine for my stay on the island. The little four-place jobs with nothing but a plastic bubble up front to fall out of looked rather fragile, but the pilot assured me they are the safest thing in the air, after which he had to boot it twice with his foot to get it started. A few minutes later he deposited me on the deck of the cruiser for a pleasant reunion. The last time I'd performed on the U.S.S. *Los Angeles* was in 1952 when she was parked in Long Beach Harbor.

The *Los Angeles* has a complement of a thousand men, and the seaplane tender *Kenneth Whiting*, parked on the other side of the dock, carries another seven hundred and fifty—so we did two shows.

I was a little apprehensive during the filming of our first show on the fantail of the *Los Angeles* because of the large group of Marines surrounding our cameramen with loaded carbines. For a while I thought it was a road company of the Musicians Union. It later developed that they were to ride herd over the cameramen to make sure the Regulus 1 Missile mounted and action-poised on the stern was not in focus. Naturally, they didn't want it shown on a TV show because General Motors would have it rolling on the freeways before the Navy could get it in the air.

As was our custom, we tried to do special material slanted at the group we were working to. I opened by telling them I'd just come from Hawaii—the most difficult spot in the world to leave—everywhere else they wave good-bye with their hands.

"My grandfather was a Naval hero. He once shouted, 'I have not yet begun to fight.' And you know, he never did. You probably remember him—Admiral Tuna, the chicken of the sea?

"The food on this ship must be terrific. I've never seen such fat seagulls."

Then I'd bring out Jayne Mansfield with a line like, "I just introduced her to two pilots. It's the first time I ever saw pilots leave vapor trails—without their planes."

After a routine with Jayne, we had a funny running gag with Jerry Colonna. I'd constantly be surprised finding him in the audience dressed in the uniform of the men surrounding him. It was easy to find him, I'd just look around for a brush with lips and he was usually somewhere underneath it. Except once, they framed me by planting Jerry in a group of servicemen who had all raised Colonna mustaches. It was frightening.

This time Jerry pretended to be one of the sailors on the boat. "What's your job?" I asked. "I polish the brass," he said. "I've got the shiniest captain in the fleet." He told me he liked being in the Navy—great spirit—everybody is "Mister." I said there might be even more spirit if a few of them were "Mrs."

We did the show in the true tradition of the Navy. I thought any minute I might have to go down with the jokes.

At this point I want to deny a rumor that Hedda Hopper asked the captain if the ship could be turned around so that the sunlight would create a halo effect in her hair. Hedda never pulls rank. What she did ask was if the island could be turned around.

After Hedda we brought Erin O'Brien on. Mansfield is

Seoul, Korea—Erin O'Brien, Hedda Hopper, and Col. Glenn's grand-father. Hedda wanted to wear the bubble home. (NBC photo by Gerald K. Smith)

meat and drink to the boys, but Erin is a delicious hunk of femininity, an awful lot like the girl next door, if you happened to be terribly lucky with neighbors. While Erin sang, we got some of the most memorable footage of the trip, and if you saw our TV show, you probably remember it—just head close-ups of individual sailors watching her. I can't describe it—who told you to miss the program.

Following the three-hour show on the boat, we went to Sukiran to do an outdoor show for the Marines at Okinawa's Camp Courtney. These guys live in tents in remote training areas called "boondocks" and train under actual battle conditions, so I did jokes that they'd particularly appreciate:

"Pretty rugged out here. Anybody that's alive after two days gets a good conduct medal.

"I hear one Marine rolled out of his lean-to this morning and shaved three times before he realized he was staring into a bear.

"You think you've got it tough here? We all had to take shots before leaving home. Les and his band went back for seconds."

The first Sputnik was big news at the time and made great material. I'd open with, "I have news from home about the race for outer space. So far only the Russians and Bing have made it."

I don't think anybody has to be reminded that at the time Bing was about to become a daddy again. After thirteen years. That's the longest coffee break on record.

That night we did another show in an enormous gymnasium at Stilwell Field. And still later in the evening Jayne Mansfield became the first American movie star to make a personal appearance at an Okinawan movie theatre. Over a thousand pushing, jostling fans packed the Kokuei Theatre in downtown Naha where one of Jayne's pictures happened to be playing. Kotara Kokuba, reputedly the richest man on Okinawa, was so grateful for Jayne's appearance that he threw a lavish feast at one of his teahouses—complete with

Ooh! Look *at that moon.* (*NBC photo*)

dancing girls doing things Arthur Murray never taught them—although I was too pooped by this time to even watch my sukiyaki.

Early next morning we were treated to a stirring sight as seven thousand Marines marched onto the baseball field to watch our show. I haven't seen that many men on third base since Babe Herman played for the Dodgers. We not only entertained them, they entertained us, and I realized that you've never really understood the meaning of the words until you've heard a Marine choir on a lonely outpost in Okinawa singing, "There Is Nothing Like a Dame."

There is a wire fence surrounding the ball field, and pasted up against it like a painted backdrop were the children of Okinawa. They looked like kids anywhere else would with their noses flattened against the bakery store window, and I was quite flattered that my style of humor could so affect them till I noticed they weren't watching me at all. Their eyes were glued on the box lunches being handed out to the cast. I guess I wasn't the only one who noticed because I attribute the great show we did that day to a belief that actors work best when they're hungry. Then, as dessert for the knothole set, I introduced a seventeen-year-old Okinawan beauty by the name of Sumiko Yosayama who sang rock and roll tunes that she'd learned phonetically from listening to jukeboxes. She stoned them, although she had no idea what she was singing about. Rock and roll must be a universal language.

A routine the servicemen everywhere loved went particularly well in this spot. I brought out Alan Gifford, a fine actor, who's worked with me all over the world. This time, Alan was dressed as a dapper Air Force general who welcomed me to the base, and offered all sorts of hospitality until I introduced him to Jayne Mansfield. Gifford is about a head shorter than Jayne and from the moment he met her, his West Point training was apparent—he'd keep his eyes straight forward. While she pitched at him, he completely forgot that I was alive, and when I'd try to interrupt, he'd put me down curtly. The sight of this well-trained example of discipline dissolving into just another human being flipped the GIs.

Our invasion of Japan was accomplished in true Air Force tradition—a pair of interceptor jets met us at 20,000 feet and made like Pepsi-Cola skywriters. They did barrel rolls, loops, dives, and often came close enough to scratch the paint. It gives you a feeling of excitement and warmth to see the interceptors buzz out to lead us in. In Washington these are billed as routine training flights, but in our hearts we knew that what their jet stream was spelling out was "Welcome! We're up here to say 'hello' and tell you there's a lot of guys waiting for you down below."

Our first stop in Japan was Itazuke Air Base in Kyushu where twenty-five hundred servicemen and their families roared their welcome to the accompaniment of the screaming F-100 jets overhead. Just as we'd arrived there'd been a jet scramble with our guys hustling into their planes as if it were a real thing—you never know when it might be. Since Pearl Harbor no blip on a radarscope has gone uninvestigated and nobody was taking any chances that this blip might only have been an echo from Jayne Mansfield.

I stepped up on the stage to murder them with some specially designed goodies and was speechless. Barney had the first idiot card printed entirely in Japanese. It broke me up. All I could say was, "A funny thing happened to me on the way to the Geisha house," and the audience laughed like they were in on the gag with McNulty.

In Tokyo we were billeted at the Imperial Hotel. I hadn't been there since 1950 and I just wanted to check and see if my shirts were back from the laundry. In Japan, you can get a shirt made to order faster than they can launder one.

The first thing I noticed as I walked into my suite was a beautiful coat of arms on the wall with an ancient Japanese motto printed underneath. At least that's what I thought it was. Turned out to be "Forget Pearl Harbor."

The service at the Imperial is the finest I've encountered anywhere. There was a button next to my bed marked ROOM SERVICE—and a maid to press it for me. The help is very polite. They bow so much, you don't know which end to talk to. And it's very disconcerting to find somebody hissing even before you've told a joke. You order a Scotch and soda and four bellhops come to your room. One carries Scotch, second carries soda, third carries ice, and the fourth arrives emptyhanded—he's just there for the tip.

The money's so complicated, even the Japanese don't understand it. I was having a great time till I ran out of my Cleveland bus tokens.

But the accommodations were very lush and comfortable. The bath in my suite was big enough to float a Buick. It even came equipped with a special back scrubber. I had a heck of a job trying to talk her out of it. The Japanese regard the bath as a kind of community activity—sort of like a P.T.A. meeting. Feeling around for the soap you're just as likely to come up with two people you didn't even know were in there. But it does eliminate the line outside the bathroom door, and keyhole spotters are unheard of. After all, who's gonna settle for a little television screen when Cinerama's available.

The telephone service is charming. In place of the usual irritating busy signal, they pipe in soothing music. Les Brown's band auditioned for the job, but were turned down. Sounded too much like the busy signal.

Soon after we'd checked in, Les burst into my room with the electrifying news that he'd found the greatest eating place in Tokyo—the Diamond Hotel. Turned out to be a Chinese restaurant. Mansfield said she'd like to try some of that Japanese rice wine—you know, sukiyaki. No one bothered to correct her. They were too busy looking.

We were in a hurry to finish dinner as we had a show to

do at Yokohama, so we took cabs back to the hotel. Tokyo cab drivers are all ex-kamikaze pilots and you haven't really lived till you've ridden with them and sometimes very shortly thereafter. Most of them speak no English at all and intricate charades are necessary to make them understand where you want to go. One night I stepped into a cab at the Imperial Hotel and was driven to four different places I didn't want to go before I uttered the one word he understood—"Imperial." He drove me back to the hotel where I stepped into another cab hoping I'd have better luck.

At Fryar Gymnasium in Yokohama we did another show for a few thousand of our enthusiastic Far Eastern personnel. Carol Jarvis, the popular young rock and roll singer, was a particular smash here and I accused her of having relatives in the audience. It's amazing how fast the hit records make it to the jukeboxes at our bases and these guys had heard Carol's latest.

That night we relaxed for an hour in one of Tokyo's larger nightclubs, Benibashi's, which features an American-type floor show and hundreds of hostesses of various nationalities. Some of the mixed racial strains are quite interesting. I saw one pretty Chinese-Hungarian eating goulash with chopsticks. Sort of an oriental Zsa Zsa Gabor. The Japanese girls refer to Occidentals as "round-eyes," which is a pretty cute way of getting even.

Marlon Brando had just finished shooting his picture when we were there and any mention of *Sayonara* drew big laughs. I think in the Japanese version of *Madame Butterfly* it's the lieutenant who's having the baby and she leaves him.

We drove back to the hotel along the Ginza, which is a lot like the main drag in any of our bigger cities. Sort of a barefoot Broadway. The Japanese are either very susceptible or very much afraid of the common cold and so many of them walk through the streets wearing surgeons masks

Jerry showing "Ace" Joe Foss how to drive on the freeway.

that you expect any minute to hear a call on the loud-speaker, "Dr. Fu Manchu wanted in surgery."

Early the next morning, we were hustled to Tachikawa Air Base, twenty-three miles east of Tokyo. Tachikawa was a Japanese Air Base during the war. When the Americans took it over after the 1945 surrender, there were only three blackened buildings standing on it.

Congress had just cut the budget for all the armed services which furnished me a very timely topic. I told them how seriously the Air Force would be affected. They were gonna have to let go all generals over twenty-five.

"And you'll have to cut down many essential services. From now on a bomber will only carry one stewardess.

"The Navy has been affected even more seriously. I know one poor admiral who had to go on a shake-down cruise in his own bathtub. He's the one who cabled, 'Sighted soap, sank same.'

"And that reminds me, nobody's allowed to send telegrams any more. Commanding officers are cautioned to go through their Christmas cards carefully—war may have been declared.

"If you think the budget cuts are serious here, you should have seen the Army-Navy game this year. The Army mule was missing. So was the Navy goat. And the hot dogs had a funny taste."

That afternoon we moved to Johnson Air Base to do an outdoor show at Walker-Schade Stadium. One of the pieces we did here was the spy sketch. I played the part of a serviceman about to embark on a six-hour pass. The sketch opens with the CO warning us that we are in a dangerous area full of spies and that we are to be on our guard—no drinking and no women. I demand to see the chaplain. If I'm gonna be dead for six hours, I want a military funeral. Needless to say, thirty seconds later I am surrounded by Jayne Mansfield playing a luscious Mata Hari for whom I'm being an overeager security risk. It was a part every man in front of us could identify with and enjoy. I kind of liked it a bit myself.

Later that night, on the way back, I kept my face glued to the car window soaking up a few final impressions of Tokyo . . . The niagara of neon signs dotting the Ginza . . . the sleepy swans floating in the moat that surrounds the Emperor's tremendous estate . . . TV antennas atop thatched huts whose tenants can't afford glass and stick paper in their windows to keep the cold out . . . The slant-eyed Santa Clauses on the street corners . . . and in the still of the night, the soft pitter-patter of feet in the hallway. It was the band trying to sneak out of the hotel with their luggage.

CHAPTER EIGHT

Back on the plane for our flight to Korea on Christmas Eve, we were delighted to find that the MATS crew had decorated the ship with mistletoe and a small Christmas tree, and suddenly I felt at home. Lately, just about the only home I've had around Christmastime has been a MATS plane. The only thing that surprised me was the strange place they found to hang the mistletoe.

We were approaching the climax of our tour and everybody was keyed up for it. Back in Los Angeles when we'd applied for our visas, the Korean Consulate had asked for two references living in Korea. The only one of our group who could comply was Betty Voigt, a *Newsweek* correspondent who was covering the trip with us and looking forward to the opportunity of visiting the birthplace of her parents.

Korea is a bleak, unyielding country saddled with grinding poverty. The destructiveness of the war is everywhere in evidence. And yet the uneasy truce, although bringing an end to the hostilities, is hardly less cruel, since it separates the predominantly industrial North from the barely subsisting agricultural South. People live in caves and mud huts, gathering scraps of wood to get through the night. Trees are a rare luxury. Men walk along the roads bearing huge stacks of twigs on their heads. It occurs to you that everybody looks like Van Cliburn but you don't mention it.

Looking down into the mountainous terrain, I marveled at the fortitude of the South Korean farmers. Through hard work and persistent labor they manage each year to reap a

Caviar to a ham. Seoul, Korea. (Official USAF photo)

large crop of rocks. At home we have farmers troubled by dust storms and drought, but these are mere irritations compared to the poor Korean who keeps falling out of his cornfield. I saw very few marks of battle in the farming country. I guess it takes more than a Commie five-hundred-pounder to take a divot out of that topsoil. Lucky our pilot was a veteran, though. He made a perfect three-bounce landing.

Stepping out of the plane, I finally figured out why the Koreans wear those weird-looking double-decker hats. The upper deck has a rock in it to keep him from blowing away.

Jayne Mansfield was next off the plane and she drew

quite a crowd. It surprised me a little. I didn't think a couple of hills more or less would be a novelty to a Korean.

We were set to jeep into Seoul when I discovered Jerry Colonna was missing. Turned out he wasn't really missing. I just didn't recognize him. He had tucked the ends of his mustache into his mouth to keep it from freezing. I laughed so hard the brassie mitten fell off my nose.

Actually, it was one of Korea's milder days. Only a few days earlier it was 7 below. Since practically the whole complement of Kimpo Air Base had turned out to say hello, it didn't seem fair to leave without doing some kind of a show. So the troupe climbed aboard a flat-bed truck and we did forty minutes of loud yelling. With no microphones to help, most of us were at a disadvantage—except Professor Colonna. His high note at the end of "Ebb Tide" had the boys running for the air-raid shelters.

After the show, we were a pretty chilly group as our little caravan tailed behind the "follow-me" jeep into Seoul. But I warmed up when I discovered that almost half the population had turned out to see us. It was very touching to see some of the younger citizens run out to our slow-moving jeeps, shake hands, grab a gas can, steal a spare tire and swipe the pen I was all set to autograph with. This was our first experience with the "Slickee Boys" of Seoul, the most accomplished sneak thieves in the world. They thought *West Side Story* was a comedy.

General George H. Decker, Commander-in-Chief of the UN Command told me that the average wage in South Korea is ninety-two dollars a year. No wonder they steal.

They tell a story about a GI who had ventured into the off-limits section of the town against the advice of his buddies. He returned triumphantly an hour later, his hand with a vise-like grip on his blouse pocket. "Well, I still got my wallet," he bragged. But his pants were missing.

Seoul is an ancient city and many of its edifices erected back in the fifth century are still standing. Which brings me

Korea. Wire flowers ahead—it's safer. (U. S. Army photo)

to the hotel we stopped at, which shall be nameless. Actually, in terms of Korean culture, it was a modern hotel, built during the reign of Genghis Khan by a rising young architect named Hilton, the Conqueror.

We spent Christmas Eve giving a performance for General Decker's UN forces in Seoul's International Theatre. This was a modern civilian movie house, its only concession to old Korean tradition being the dressing-room chairs which were nailed to the floor.

I know I endeared myself forever in the hearts of those Seoul-based servicemen when I led off with:

"You fellows certainly came a long way to avoid the draft.

"Nice healthy climate you've got. All the diseases do well here.

"You know, with the Sputniks and intercontinental missiles, the people back home are so nervous, it's a pleasure to be out here in this rest area.

"We had lots of fun flying over. What laughs! Coming into Pearl Harbor we had the pilot ask for landing instructions in Japanese.

"What a reception we got. I thought I'd die!"

We were invited to a reception that night at the brand-new officers' club, and most of the cast were scouring the town for Christmas presents to exchange with one another. They picked up beautiful hand-hammered ashtrays and intricately carved opium pipes for next to nothing. The big blow came when we tried to buy Christmas wrapping paper. It developed that the paper was in such low supply and such high demand that in most cases it exceeded the price paid for the present. When the gifts were exchanged, Hedda wound up with the prize package. Some sneak had presented her with a knitted shawl neatly wrapped around four sheets of Christmas paper. "That's all for now, Hedda. See you tomorrow."

Early Christmas Day, we boarded a fleet of twenty passenger tandem rotor helicopters and were transported from Seoul to Bayonet Bowl. This trip by auto over the rocky Korean terrain would have taken three hours. In the banana choppers it was twenty-five minutes. Our pilot made the trip memorable by pointing out the 38th Parallel below—much too close and almost directly below—and informing us that if we ventured north of it, we would be fired upon. And the colonel who supervised our landing did nothing to ease the tension by casually remarking, "We've never had so many men congregated in one spot. It would be just like those bastards to come over and bomb us today."

One of the biggest thrills of the Far Eastern tour was meeting Cardinal Spellman in Seoul. I had never met the Cardinal before although I had worked for him in several of his New York Catholic Charity shows along with Bing, Jimmy Durante, Ann Blythe, Ruth Hussey, and many others.

I had breakfast with His Eminence at Major General Thomas J. Sands' headquarters on Christmas morning and I found out that the Cardinal has a great sense of humor. All his retinue got quite a kick out of our ad-lib session.

We shook hands and I said, "Cardinal, it's amazing how far we had to travel before we finally met." And the Cardinal said, "Yes, and I'm glad we're not in competition for audiences over here." I'll take his Trendex for mine any time. After all, look at the sponsor he's got.

The Cardinal said, "I understand we're playing some of the same spots." And I said, "Yes, I play them first and then you come after me and give the troops absolution."

Later, when I introduced Al Sharper to the Cardinal, I explained that Al was the editor of *Daily Variety*, the show business bible. The Cardinal smiled and said, "I'm very pleased to meet you, sir, I work for the other Bible."

The USO has decorated the Cardinal for his many wonderful Christmas jaunts to all parts of the world to help bring our boys moral and spiritual enlightenment.

The sight of seven thousand GIs of the 7th Infantry Division perched on a hillside among the snowdrifts to watch us perform at the Bayonet Bowl in Korea on Christmas Day packed enough emotion into this unsentimental frame to last a lifetime. Only the plaintive voice of Hedda Hopper inquiring as to the whereabouts of the closest powder room saved me from indulging in a maudlin exhibition of eye-blinking. One of my more hard-boiled writers remarked that I refrained from tears only because I didn't want to soak the idiot cards.

Here were thousands of American men—some of them still

Okinawa. Some who forgot to make reservations. (NBC photo)

faking it with a razor and soft stubble of peach fuzz—too
many miles away from home and family—with a temporary
leave of absence from their foxholes—roaring with apprecia-
tion when a middle-aged comedian said:

"Here we are in Korea. The Miami Beach of the Far East.

"How about this weather? All day long my undies have
been creeping up looking for a place to hide.

"And if they find one, I'm gonna crawl in myself.

"I don't want to start any rumors, but I think there's a
spy up here. I saw a fellow with a tan.

"They don't bother with roll call here . . . No sense counting noses, nobody's got one."

They were fairly routine cold-weather jokes, but those kids were still able to laugh at their own plight. I really hit them where they lived when I said:

"In a climate like this you don't need a marriage ceremony . . . You just wet your lips, kiss the girl, and till death do you part!"

It's a tribute to a GI's philosophy that he can appreciate humor of that sort. Put him in a foxhole, on the side of a barren mountain, with practically inaccessible trails, and he's still got hopes that maybe some lost chick will pop in beside him just to get warm.

It had been nine months since the last USO show passed their way and these boys were starved for entertainment . . . Their buddies—the ones who had caught that show of almost a year ago—were watching the store in the rifle pits along the 38th Parallel facing the Communist North.

This was an easy audience—but I don't think any of us ever worked harder or enjoyed it more. Erin O'Brien's act was interrupted when a voice with just a touch of the brogue yelled, "My name is Tom Coughlin." To which Erin replied, "A fine Irish boy like you deserves a kiss." Whereupon she planted one on his cheek. In no time at all the place sounded like a camp full of Pat O'Briens.

The weather was close to freezing and working on an open stage was particularly tough on Les Brown's boys. Take the brass section—they'd blow a chorus, then have to wait an extra chorus before they could unpucker and get their instruments loose.

Hedda Hopper did her question and answer stint wearing just a thin lace shawl. We were congratulating her on her fortitude when she revealed she was wearing four or five dresses at the same time.

I even got a little unearned applause when the boys

thought I had joined Arthur Duncan in his dance act. Actually, I was just stomping around trying to get warm.

Erin O'Brien closed the show with the usual "White Christmas," but this time she had the real backdrop to go with it.

Two hours later, in the gathering winter gloom, we choppered over to 1st Cavalry Division Headquarters to entertain in a similar setting.

Certain things are burned into your memory sort of like the after-image you get closing your eyes when you've been looking into a bright light. In Korea, it was the faces of the men at Wallenstein Bowl. We didn't get there till early afternoon and these guys had been sitting there since nine in the morning. They came early to get a good seat in the snow.

These are the kind of shows that tell the whole story, the big reason why these trips have to be made. It's great to entertain the boys in Hawaii or Tokyo, or Yokohama, but when you see these combat troops squatting in the snow, hungry for any break in their drab routine, you feel like you're in the right racket.

It was five below zero that Christmas morning and the members of the cast, as I introduced them, would break away from their huddle around the coffee urn backstage and come on to do their act. We did a long show in spite of the warning by our chopper pilots that the fog rolls in thick and fast as soon as the late afternoon shadows fall.

Every time I'd come to a line I thought I might get off with, I'd notice the eyes of the men following the members of our cast and crew as one by one they were hustled off to the waiting banana copters. It was a little like the look you see on the faces of people at airports and railroad stations seeing other people off, or on the faces of your kids when you tell them you're going out for the evening—only you know this is gonna be one of those real long evenings. I'd

What a switch. Jayne Mansfield's back. Wallenstein Bowl, Korea.
(NBC photo by Gerald K. Smith)

start another routine, and another, and the shadows were getting longer.

The crew of the last chopper feeling their way through the foggy cabin counted noses and one that would have been obvious to find was missing. They marked it down to the ham in me that wouldn't let me get off, and led me away shouting a last punch-line into the fog. I turned to the pilot and said, "Okay, let's go. Which way is Seoul?" He said, "Who knows now?"

Seeing the look of shock on my face, he was quick to reassure me. "Don't worry," he said, "we've got the best natural compass in the world here. We just take off and fly for three minutes and if they start shooting at us, we know we've drifted north over the 38th Parallel—but fasten your seat belt. I think we'll make it."

We were a mighty weary group gathered at the Yokota Air Base outside of Tokyo, waiting to make the last leg of our journey home, and in the half-light of the early dawn our plane appeared a bit pooped, too. My eyes were deceiving me, of course, but I had the distinct impression that our stratocruiser was about to take off from a kneeling position. I was ready to climb on board and forget the whole thing, but the chicken in me took over and I asked our pilot if our ship didn't appear a little tailheavy. He nodded wearily. "Your cast's been Christmas shopping," he said, "and unless we unload a few knickknacks, we may not have room for the co-pilot."

I felt guilty about the stone Buddha I picked up in Tokyo for practically twice what it was worth, and a few other little trinkets I had packed into a large warehouse case, and I was about to confess when I was interrupted by a timely tap on the shoulder. It was General C. G. Lessig, Commander of Andersen Air Force Base, asking me if I would mind including a few lonely soldiers on Guam in our itinerary. It wasn't too far out of the way, and the chance to ride on one of those SAC B-47 jets helped make up my

On stage Christmas day at Bayonet Bowl in Korea. What a hand I got when the girls came out. (NBC photo by Gerald K. Smith)

Pyongyang–Korea. I stopped to count the house. (NBC photo)

mind. It would give me a chance to get there earlier, set up the show, and my little Buddha wouldn't get bumped.

You should have seen old Dad sitting up there in the observer's seat with oxygen mask, crash helmet, and chute. I looked like the straight man in a Milton Berle sketch. Felt just as risky, too. Nobody to talk to. It was like sitting in the electric chair waiting for them to turn the power on.

We weren't in the air very long before I began getting that closed-in feeling. I couldn't see anything in front of me but a panel of instruments, and a little stream of sweat was fogging my eyeballs.

The pilot of the B-47, a fellow Californian, Captain James Stillson of Berkeley, told me to take off my parachute and lie down in the narrow catwalk and get a couple of hours of shut-eye, which I did. When I opened my eyes, the captain was shaking me. He said, "Crawl up in the co-pilot's seat and you'll see why I'm still in this business."

The co-pilot seat is directly behind the pilot. I pulled myself up into it and took a look at the sun dancing on the beautiful cloud formations. It was a magnificent sight even in my condition. As we cruised along at six hundred miles per hour, the captain said, "If you want to see a little better, just pull the lever on the right-hand side and it'll raise your seat." I reached down and pulled a red knob and nothing happened. I said, "You mean this lever with the red knob?"

"For blank sake, get your hand off that!" he yelled. "It's the ejector knob." I looked under the seat for a container. We were eight hundred miles out in the Pacific. It's a good thing they have a protective device on that knob or this would have been the last chapter in the book.

The rest of the 1900-mile flight to Guam was uneventful. We made it in a little over three and a half hours, and I spent most of that time shaking hands with my St. Christopher medal. No one but the pilot knew how close television came to losing another comedian. When we touched down, I got off the plane in my crash helmet swinging a golf club, but I'm afraid my swing was a little shaky.

When the liaison officer suggested a visit to the Naval Hospital, I thought I must be showing the strain, but what he had in mind was a little informal chitchat with the patients—boys who wouldn't be able to see the show we had planned. I toured the wards telling a joke here, laying an egg there for an hour or so. I'd have stayed longer, but they told me they needed the bed.

Back at the BOQ assigned to me, I had another example of that good old Air Force hospitality. Right there on the dresser was the usual bottle of Dr. I. W. Harper's pain-killer, along with his nephew, Johnnie Walker. I won't say I was overanxious, but I think I had two drinks before I got the cork out of the bottle. By the time the rest of the cast arrived, Johnny Pawlek had laid out the stage, put up the mikes, and re-starched my spine.

We were working at Gilkerson Field, which is a football stadium between USO shows, and the general's "few lonesome men on Guam" turned out to be 12,000—the largest audience we played to on the tour. It was a beautiful sunny day and the frostbite I collected in Korea wound up with a nice even tan.

Talk about tropical atmosphere—this place had everything—banyan trees, breadfruit, coconuts, even a turquoise lagoon. If Bing was along, we'd have had another "Road" picture without even building a set.

Personally, I'm no stranger to the South Pacific. I'd been there twice before and I've got the fungus to prove it.

But I was grateful to the Defense Department for their vote of confidence. It was the first time in four years that they let me bring my act to a warm climate. That's what I was referring to when I told this large group of airmen:

"The Defense Department insisted I play here. It's been a long time since you fellows have seen any action and they wanted to see if you could still take it.

"They were going to send Jack Benny, but Jack's sick. He had a terrible accident. His electric blanket short-circuited and four thousand dollars went up in smoke.

"Jack has the only Sealy mattress in the world with a burglar alarm."

And a few more that I'm now too chicken to remember . . . But I still retain the mental picture of Guam with its coconut trees on the slopes, the turquoise lagoon in the valley, and the heavy stone Buddha in the bathroom of the BOQ where I was quartered. I hated to leave old Pudgy, but our C-97's pilot said it was either him or me.

We were taking the scenic route home and heading for Kwajalein, that tiny speck in the Pacific known as "the world's most expensive gas station" . . . It was to be a quickie—just one show while they were refueling our box lunches—and we had almost a whole hour to do with as we pleased while they set up the stage. I spent my time strolling barefoot along the coral-strewn beach collecting specimens for my son Kelly's shell collection. I really hit the jackpot. In no time at all I had collected a large sack of assorted shells, a two-inch cut on my big toe, and a bad case of sunburn. I lugged my trophies back to my quarters, dumped them on the bed, stripped to my shorts and went to work on my wounds with Mercurochrome and Unguentine. Hedda Hopper chose that moment to enter and greeted me with a quiet scream of horror.

"Come on now, Hedda," I said, "Mickey Hargitay shows more skin than this just by unbuttoning his collar."

"It isn't that, Bob," she said, almost speechless. Well, it's almost speechless for Hedda. She had her eyes averted and was pointing a shaking finger at my bed. "Look," she said.

I glanced over at my collection of beach debris and couldn't believe my eyes. Four of my "sea shells" had risen up on long hairy legs and were walking across the pillow!

I'm glad the door was wide enough because Hedda and I made it in a dead-heat. My clothing would still be molding in that quiet little cottage on Kwajalein if somebody hadn't explained to me about hermit crabs and their quaint little habit of starting a new housing development every time a snail or something moves out.

Back at Hickam Field sometime after midnight, a bedraggled group of gypsies disembarked and looked distastefully forward to a dreary trip through customs. It might have taken hours but for the inspired stratagem of brother Jack who was at the head of the line.

As the customs inspector opened his bag and prepared to

make a detailed inspection of its contents, Jack casually cautioned, "Be careful—don't cut your hand on that coral in there." The inspector withdrew his hand as though Jack were transporting a sack of snakes, and, hurriedly scratching a chalk mark on the bag, called, "Next!" From that point on, everybody in line was bringing in practically nothing but coral. We whizzed through customs.

Approaching Burbank the following evening, we had more people in the cockpit than in the cabin. Everybody wanted to watch the landing, and with the excitement of homecoming, we were a fairly noisy and unruly group. I can only attribute our safe landing on the excessive skill of Captain Hal M. Terry, who during the critical moments of approach could hear nothing of the vital information being shouted to him by his co-pilot and flight engineer.

Dolores and the kids were waiting on the runway with a Christmas tree and presents and we had a belated celebration on the spot from which twelve days and seventeen thousand miles earlier we'd left. I turned to Doc Shurr, my agent, and said, "I've been back in California for a full two minutes. Surely you can dig up a benefit for me to do tonight."

The Doctor doesn't understand jokes. An hour later I was at the Biltmore Hotel doing a dinner honoring the two football teams that would play in the Rose Bowl New Year's Day. As I remember it, I started out with, "I was quite an athlete in college . . . you've heard of the 'Fordham Flash' . . . I was the Cleveland Creep. I was a great player, shifting, bucking, weaving. I moved around so much, nobody would sit on the same bench with me."

And as soon as the dinner was over, I did a little broken field-running on the freeway and headed for the house. There's no pad like home.

CHAPTER NINE

People ask me, "Why do you keep moving so much?"

My stock answer is, "With the kind of jokes I do, it's safer!"

But of course, I get around the way I do because there are people everywhere, and to me, people are audiences and I love audiences. Swift and Company never put out a bigger ham than I am. With the possible exception of Jack Benny, who loves the business, loves audiences, and will work anywhere from a gas-station rest room to the Philharmonic. There are not enough people like him in show business—a good audience is therapy to him.

Jack's so hammy, if his sink gurgles, he does twenty minutes. It took him two weeks to realize that Mary wasn't along on the honeymoon. He's learning to play the violin lefty because he heard that's his good side. Jack really loves the spotlight. He had his house redone because it had indirect lighting.

With all my traveling around the globe, I've acquired a reputation for being a GI entertainer. There have been newspaper stories and magazine articles about my devotion to the GIs. Well, I do love those guys. We have a certain rapport. I know that what these guys have done took plenty of guts and courage, and they admired my act, too.

The truth of the matter is, the GIs have done a lot more for me than I've ever done for them. The servicemen are the greatest audience in the world. Wherever I've gone to entertain them, they've been kind enough to laugh at my jokes, and that's meat and potatoes to me. And dessert, too!

That's why I look forward to Christmas each year—it means another tour to entertain GIs stuck off in places that even Rand and McNally haven't found yet. And another laughter transfusion for me.

All our Christmas tours to various parts of the world have been memorable. Each trip has had its high spots, its low spots, its mishaps. The unexpected happens so often, it becomes routine.

Of all these tours, our Christmas junket of 1958 will always stand out in my mind. It was a lulu. Things happened on that trip that I never bargained for. We were scheduled to do shows for some forty thousand servicemen and their families in eight countries and cover 16,000 miles in the process.

Somewhere along those 16,000 miles, my blood pressure went AWOL, my pulse started doing the cha-cha, and I starred in a couple of blackouts that weren't in the script.

Things really piled up on me. At one point I was so knocked out, I got a get-well card from Oscar Levant. That's when I really got worried!

Of course I had no idea all this was going to happen when I got together with the Pentagon brass to map out that Christmas tour. The main objective of these conferences is to map a route that will bring entertainment to servicemen in the more remote spots. The remoter the better. At Christmas I'd rather do a show for a handful of guys stuck out in the Aleutians than for forty thousand GIs at home.

Our '58 tour was to take in bases and military installations in the Azores, North Africa, Spain, Italy, Germany, and Iceland. We were to take twelve days. As my eye ran down the list of cities and stops we were to make, it looked easy enough. I was to discover later that the only way you can cover all that territory in so short a time is to leave from Cape Canaveral.

For this tour we had Hedda Hopper, Jerry Colonna, Molly Bee, Elaine Dunne, Randy Sparks, and of course Les

I'd walk a mile for a taxi. (Photo 7280th Air Depot Wing)

Brown and his band. In Spain we were to pick up Gina Lollobrigida.

Hedda Hopper has become a regular on our Christmas safaris. Hedda's a great trouper. She's forever gay, effervescent, with a smile for everyone. After a long plane flight that leaves the rest of us limp, Hedda skips off the plane looking as bright, fresh, and crisp as though she'd just stepped out of *Vogue*.

I was a little worried about Hedda on the first trip she made with us. As I helped her aboard the plane, I wondered if I'd done the right thing in inviting a grandmother on a grueling twenty-thousand-mile tour. I needn't have worried. At the end of the trip, when we landed back in Los Angeles, Hedda took my arm and helped *me* down the steps. I don't know where Hedda gets her energy, but that gal sure gets a lot out of her Wheaties.

I've made very few excursions without my old pal Professor Jerry Colonna. Velour Lip has traveled hundreds of thousands of miles with me. The Mad Professor is as familiar to GIs around the globe as C rations, but a lot more welcome.

Colonna always kills the audience. The Professor doesn't just sing a song, he fractures it. He lambastes it like a butcher pounding a tough sirloin. His piercing high note is pretty terrifying; it sounds like the mating call of a pair of corduroy pants. We don't let the Professor hit high C in the Arctic, it attracts timber wolves. Jerry was singing in stereophonic sound long before it was invented.

Having Professor Colonna along on our tours is a real comfort to me. It's good to know that no matter what strange countries we may visit and what weird species we may be confronted with, we've got something to match it.

And what a traveler! You've heard of people falling asleep the moment they get on a plane? Colonna beats that—he has to be carried aboard. The Professor is such a sound sleeper, on several trips he's gone as baggage.

Another standby of our tours is Les Brown and his band. If space permitted, I could write several chapters about these wonderful guys. They all deserve medals for performances above and beyond the call of Local 47. To help put on our shows, these fellows have played in most of the countries of the world, often under rough conditions. I'll always have a special niche in my affections for Les and his musical wetbacks.

To start our tour, certain machinery has to be set in motion. First, we have to have planes to fly us where we're

A couple of beautiful maps. (NBC photo)

going. You can't play eight countries in twelve days traveling by bus.

MATS, which means Military Air Transport Service, provided us with a couple of C-118s, complete with pilots and crews. At one time or another, almost every guy in the Armed Services has flown by MATS and as a consequence we have a ball kidding about their planes. On this trip we used lines like, "We flew up here in a 118. That's not the model number—that's the year it was built. The 'No Smoking' sign was in Latin. We thought they were kidding until the pilot came on wearing a toga and sandals."

Les Brown's band in Korea—just before they defected to the bar. *(Photo by Jerry Holscher)*

On other trips we used, "I don't know how old the plane was, but Lindbergh's lunch was still on the seat. The path to the washroom was outside." Or, "The Air Force went all out for us. They gave us a plane that belonged to a four-star General . . . Pershing!" But I kid with crossed fingers: the MATS guys and gals have given up a lot of time off to ferry us safely all over the globe.

The next item was passports. Every member of our troupe must have his passport in order and validated for all the countries we're going to visit. I've traveled so much, my passport is practically in shreds. It's been stamped and re-stamped so often, the picture in it is beginning to look like me.

For the next step, we all reported to the Army Medical Center for overseas shots. Shots for typhus, typhoid, diphtheria, tetanus, and cholera. Everyone hates this part of the routine. After the doctor had stuck the needle in my arm for the fifth or sixth time, I said, "Aren't you overdoing it?" He said, "Oh, excuse me. In civilian life I was a tattoo artist!"

"17 December. Depart Burbank Airport 9 A.M."
That was the top line in the mimeoed schedule of our itinerary. And at 9 A.M. on December 17 some sixty people gathered at Burbank Airport for our departure. This number included our cast, the members of the orchestra, and our technicians. To the passers-by we must have looked like a small mob scene.

After the newsreels and photographers from the Los Angeles papers had taken a few pictures, we got aboard our planes. Alongside the runway stood our wives and families, waving good-bye, and wondering what kind of nuts they had married. To those of our group making a tour for the first time, this was an exciting moment. As our planes roared off the runway and started their climb over the Sierra Mountains, I noticed Molly Bee and Randy Sparks and the other youngsters aboard looking down at the San Fernando Valley dropping rapidly away behind us, and I could guess what was going through their minds. This was it—they'd go halfway around the world before they saw that valley and their homes again. I understood how they felt; I never started one of those trips without that strange sense of excitement.

Our first stop was McGuire Air Force Base at Fort Dix, near Trenton, New Jersey. We were scheduled to have dinner and immediately take off for the Azores. But the second plane developed engine trouble and had been forced to land at Edwards Air Force Base back in California. We stayed overnight till they caught up with us, then took off the next morning at 7 A.M.

At McGuire we'd been joined by a contingent of newspaper people from New York. The press and magazines must've considered our trip newsworthy; they sent some of their top writers to cover it. Eleanor Harris represented *McCall's*; Atra Baer the Hearst newspapers; John Reddy on assignment from the *Reader's Digest*; Mel Opotowsky of United Press International; Jay Miller of NBC, New York; Dave Smith and Paul Bailey from NBC, Hollywood; and of course Ursula Halloran from New York. I've already mentioned the redoubtable Hedda Hopper, who would file her syndicated column every day while en route. To round out the group, there was Frank Liberman who takes care of my press and publicity on the Coast.

I haven't seen such a concentration of newshawks in one place outside of Liz Taylor's patio.

I got to know this bunch very well on our tour. Atra Baer is the daughter of the late "Bugs" Baer whose unique brand of humor has delighted newspaper readers for three decades. Atra, following in her father's celebrated footsteps, is a top feature writer for the New York *Journal-American* and other Hearst papers across the country.

Eleanor Harris of *McCall's* is an old friend of mine. She has interviewed me in my home in North Hollywood, and now here she was reporting on me in my natural habitat, a plane.

John Reddy is another friend of long standing. John is a first-rate journalist and reporter, no fact ever escapes him. I never saw him without a pencil in his hand, taking notes.

NBC's "Monitor" program wanted some taped interviews with GIs along our route. Jay Miller was on hand with his tape recorder to fill the bill. Jay had that tape rolling constantly and he could blackmail us all.

I didn't know Mel Opotowsky of UPI, but we got well acquainted during the tour. Mel has given me some fine breaks in his articles.

But during that 1958 Christmas tour I got some world-wide publicity that I'd rather have done without. And in the most unspectacular way—I got sick.

People often ask me, "How do you keep up this terrific pace?" And I always answer, "I thrive on it." Which is true —show business is exciting, colorful, fast-moving—it's the rat race I love. Some guys are happy pumping gasoline, or selling shoes, or delivering milk; me, I like to stand on a stage, hurl jokes at people, and take my chances on what they hurl back.

I couldn't even imagine taking it easy, or slowing down. The day before we left on this tour, I'd flown up to Oakland to do a show for the newsboys of the Oakland *Tribune*. I'd promised my old friend Senator Knowland I'd be there and I wasn't going to disappoint him. I got home at 3 A.M., and at 7 A.M. I was at Burbank Airport preparing to take off on a 16,000-mile trip.

En route from McGuire to the Azores I got a few snatches of sleep in a plane seat, between rehearsals with the cast. The weather was stormy when we landed at the Azores, with gale winds and rain whipping us as we struggled over to the hangar for a show for the island personnel, which made my opening remarks doubly appropriate.

"It's a pleasure to be here in Honolulu. That's what they told me when they led me to the plane. What sneaks! They had all the fellows on the gas truck singing 'Aloha Oe.' They tell me you get your share of dew here. Is it true that your dress uniform is a blotter? You gotta be a fast man on a weekend pass here . . . Sit around too long and your date rusts. I know a lieutenant who got married and spent the first three weeks of his honeymoon wringing out his bride."

During this show, a strange feeling came over me. For once, I felt actually tired.

After the show and dinner, we all climbed back into our planes and took off for our next stop, Port Lyautey, North Africa.

As I dropped into my plane seat, I admitted to myself that the old bones could really use a little rest. But there was no shut-eye for any of us on that flight. Any of us, that is, but Les White. Les can make it any time. He just closes his eyes and that's it. His partner, Johnny Rapp, claims that Les dozes off in the middle of writing sessions, and keeps insisting he's awake. When Johnny points out that he has his eyes closed, he mumbles, "No, they're open—I just have the lids over them." He has even learned to wiggle a finger while fast asleep to create the impression that he's awake and thinking. Once, in England, in the middle of a writing session, Les took two wake-up tablets and went out like a light. He uses them regularly now instead of sleeping pills. How he slept through this weather, though, I'll never know. As soon as we left the Azores, we ran into thunderstorms, and the plane tossed around like a hula hoop on a belly dancer. For the first time, an airplane flight really bothered me.

After a sleepless flight, we landed at seven in the morning at Port Lyautey, Morocco.

We crawled off the plane and I headed for our quarters for a few hours of sack time. Every bone in my body ached for sleep. But it wasn't to be. Captain Jack Counihan had scheduled a charity golf match and I couldn't disappoint him. The jeeps were waiting and off we went.

By that time, I was really groggy. The sun gets pretty hot in Morocco. Before we finished playing, I was so beat I could hardly climb out of my divots. To give you an idea how exhausted I was, I put down my right score.

A golf course in the sandy terrain of Morocco is a rarity. The fairways were all sand, and every so often there was a little patch of grass—that was a trap.

I was paired with the amateur golf champs of Morocco, Bouchaib and Abdel Kadar Hadadi, and though I was pooped we won our match, quicker than you could say Bouchaib Hadadi.

During the charity golf tournament, I was just addressing the ball to tee off on the first hole, when suddenly all hell broke loose. A series of air-raid sirens went off in my ear, together with weird wailings like a flock of banshees. A wild cacophony of sounds fractured the air like the testing area of a bagpipe factory. For a moment I thought Spike Jones had parachuted in.

Then I saw where all this was coming from. A ragged group of tall, bearded, white-turbaned Berbers were standing at the edge of the green. As the noise they produced from thin clarinet-like pipes and twelve-foot horns beat through my skull, I got a glimmer of what was going on. These were brother Jack's newest "discoveries" and they were "auditioning!"

I'd never before heard anything like the Riff Mountain Boys, as the group called themselves, and I was sure no one else had either, so later as a novelty I had them on my television show. And they really were a novelty. Their music blew out tubes in sets all over America. And when they went into their high C finish, they came close to blowing out the powerhouse at Hoover Dam.

The Riff Mountain Boys were one of the high spots of our visit to Morocco. I'll never forget them. Whenever I drive by the plush headquarters of the musicians' union in Hollywood, I think of these tall, bearded tribesmen and their weird instruments. If there's any music on the moon, it probably sounds like the stuff the Riff Mountain Boys turn out.

You'll find that I mention golf quite often in these pages. I don't have to tell you that's my real racket. Movies and TV are just a sideline—something to linger with until the dew gets off the grass. I'm up every morning at the crack of my back, sweating over a hot golf ball unless the money men have me trapped in a jute mill. And it's an enthusiasm of many of my crew.

One of the best golfers in my group is Johnny Pawlek, a sound engineer, who has been with me for many years. Recently, the NBC technicians were out on strike and Pawlek was picketing in front of the studios. Sam Snead, who was doing a guest shot on my program, drove up and got out of his car. Pawlek squared his shoulders and said, "Mr. Snead, are you going to cross this picket line?" Snead said, "I'm afraid I have to." Johnny Pawlek, true to the cause he was fighting for, held up the picket sign prominently in his two hands and said, "Well, as you go by, would you mind taking a look at this grip?"

After the match at Kenitra golf course, I hurried back to our quarters at Port Lyautey with the idea of grabbing an afternoon nap. But again, no dice. I found the cast climbing into several command cars.

I said, "What's up?"

Hedda Hopper said, "We're going to Rabat to meet the Sultan, King Mohammed." That was all I had to hear. I can always take a nap, a Sultan you don't meet every day. I piled in and we were off to Rabat.

As it turned out, we didn't meet a Sultan that day either. King Mohammed hadn't been apprised of our coming—or maybe he had—and he wasn't in the palace. However, his Cabinet Chief, Abderahamane Naggai, took us in hand and showed us around the place.

The King's palace consists of a group of quite beautiful buildings, decorated with magnificent Arabic tilework. It's almost as impressive as a California gas station. As Mr. Naggai showed us around the Sultan's quarters, I kept asking, "Where's the harem?" but Mr. Naggai kept pretending not to hear me. He's not a diplomat for nothing.

Every door we went through had an armed guard standing in front of it, tough Moroccan soldiers. I asked, "Why all the guards?" Seems there's dissension among the tribes, some of whom occasionally swoop down from the hills and try to make shish kebab of their enemies.

I didn't even know Spike Jones belonged to the club. Golfing in Morocco. The greens all break toward Mecca. (NBC photo)

Fortunately, none of these skirmishes occurred while we were in Morocco. I guess the people figured, one crisis at a time.

On the way back to Lyautey, we stopped in for tea at the home of the Pasha of Kenitra, Abdel Hamid el Alaoui, a stocky, round-faced, jovial type. The Pasha laughed at every one of my jokes. I found out later he doesn't understand a word of English.

Nevertheless, when I walked out on the stage at Port Lyautey that night, there was the Pasha, smack in the front row, with an entourage of half a dozen aides. The Pasha laughed like crazy all through the show, and naturally, when he laughed, his aides laughed, too. They were a big help in putting over the show. But I've often wondered how the Pasha and his pals would have reacted if they'd understood my material. By the way, if you ever happen to be in Port Lyautey, drop in on the Pasha. He serves a great glass of mint tea.

The American Ambassador, Charles W. Yost, took us on a fast tour of Rabat, a really fascinating city. Half French, half Moroccan, it's a colorful combination of Paris and Casablanca.

We wound up in the Medina, the local Casbah, which is not recommended for tourists. Instead of taking a quiet nap, as I should have been doing, I spent the afternoon in a teeming anthill of cutthroats, pickpockets, and shady characters who'd committed every crime in the book. Including one I couldn't forgive them for—no one asked me for my autograph.

In the evening we got back to Port Lyautey. And for the first time since we left Burbank, California, I undressed and got into a real bed and slept. For exactly ninety minutes. Then they were shaking me, and I was on my way to the hangar to do our show.

All this time, a little voice was whispering, "Slow down. Don't be a fool. Idiot, you're overdoing it for a man of forty-two!" And let me tell you, I should've listened. I really should. After all, that little voice knows my *real* age.

After the show there was a big party, and naturally I had to be there. I didn't want to disappoint the CO, Captain V. A. Jennings, and the wonderful people of the base who had gone to so much trouble for us. Just as I couldn't disappoint Jack Counihan about the golf match, and the Sultan who didn't show up, and so forth. I got to bed at three-thirty A.M., and hopped up at eight A.M., bright-eyed, smiling, and punchy, and we took off for Morón, Spain.

If there's anything I hate, it's getting up early in the morning. But on this tour it wasn't much of a problem because we hardly ever went to bed.

So there I was, after four hours of sack time, standing on the Port Lyautey airstrip in the dawn's early light, saying good-bye to our wonderful hosts and fumbling my way aboard our plane.

A minute later we were in the air. We were scheduled to do a show that afternoon for the Air Force at Morón, so haste was necessary. We'd been on African soil 24 hours, and here we were on our way again, headed for Europe.

That'll give you an idea how our tours are laid out—our schedule gave us three hours to get from one continent to the next. On every tour I've undertaken, I've always sworn that when I got back home, I'd search out the guy who lays out our itineraries and beat him over the head with his own stopwatch. I once screamed at our liaison man, Colonel Layden: "Who dreamed up this crazy schedule? I'd like to say a few words to that idiot!" Colonel Layden calmly looked me in the eye and replied, "You can take it up with him any morning when you're shaving. Just look in your mirror." He went on to explain that I was the culprit. I get requests from friends stationed at various places along our route asking me to do a show for them. How do you turn down a request like that? After you write in a few of these requests into your schedule, you find yourself making more stops than a Flit salesman in a nudist colony.

At the beginning of each tour, every member of our troupe is handed a mimeoed sheet neatly printed like a timetable. Thereafter, that sheet is our bible. The line of type on my schedule for this particular day read, "*20 Dec. Fly to Morón. Afternoon Show. Fly to Madrid.*"

Traveling with a show troupe in a MATS plane is a lot different from flying on a commercial airline. We're a bunch of gypsies with wings. Everyone yaks it up, and the bon mots fly thick and fast. Even our pilot, Captain Ray Coddington, affectionately known as Smiling Jack, got into the act. As we headed for southern Europe, he came on the public address system and said, "Welcome aboard, ladies and gentlemen. We are now crossing the Mediterranean and will soon be over Spain. However, there's been a slight change in our flight plan. We will be passing over Communist East Germany, where we will participate in war games. Be calm and no one will be hurt. Thank you." Cute, huh? That's the kind of joke you laugh at while your hair is turning gray.

We were still chuckling over the captain's joke when we flew into a thunderstorm, and lightning struck the plane. The blinding flash of white light and the crackling noise as the bolt streaked through the plane had many of us thinking that the war games were on, and we'd had it!

We had designed our show for the overseas servicemen as sort of a package of news from home, presented with humor and music. And we had some very bright young talent. At Lyautey, as I'd watched the packed rows of young Navy men and their families laughing and applauding the various acts, I knew we had the right formula.

Randy Sparks is a young singer of folk songs I had first seen in the Village Vanguard in New York. In addition to being the possessor of a fine singing voice, Randy plays his own accompaniment on the guitar, a factor to be taken into consideration on our treks. We put on many of our shows in places where there's no music or even a stage, and the performer who can "go on" without a lot of props is very valuable under those conditions.

Another member of our cast was Elaine Dunne, a lovely young dancer from my home town Cleveland, who had been getting great notices in Las Vegas. I caught Elaine at the Tropicana Hotel in Las Vegas, where her great singing and sensational dancing had the gamblers deserting the casinos to watch her and applaud. I knew Elaine's youthful loveliness and fresh, vibrant personality would go over big with the servicemen.

At the time we were assembling our cast, a pert and pretty young lady who might have come right off a Norman Rockwell *Saturday Evening Post* cover was appearing on several TV shows and was a featured performer on the Tennessee Ernie show. I mean, of course, Molly Bee. Molly, although still in her teens, is a seasoned performer. She steps out on a stage and puts over a song with all the verve and aplomb of an Ethel Merman.

These three fine young performers—Molly, Elaine, and Randy—were a hit everywhere we played. It's peacetime, not wartime, that is hardest on the nerves of the GIs stationed overseas. The overseas GI is the forgotten man when there's no war going on, and he knows it. There's nothing exciting or heroic about serving out time in an enforced absence from home. This is the guy whose morale needs a lift.

And there are scores of entertainers who, through the USO, are trying to provide that lift. With or without headlines, fuss or fanfare they pack their earmuffs and grease paint every Christmas. Johnny Grant and Roscoe Ates have barnstormed with their troupe all over Korea. Gil Lamb, Dave Ketchum, Charlie Watts, and Irish McCalla hit all the bases in Europe and the Far East. Sid Marion and his gypsies crossed sled tracks with us up in Alaska. You may not recognize all these names, but they know 'em out in no-man's land and the farther you get from home base, the bigger the applause.

We touched down at Morón, Spain, on an airstrip glistening with rain and hopped puddles to the mess hall for hot coffee.

Seventy-six hours had elapsed since we'd left Burbank, California. Out of those seventy-six hours, I'd slept about seven. Now, as I shook hands with the commanding officer of Morón Air Base, Colonel Ernest Nance, something suddenly went out of kilter.

I saw the CO's welcoming smile through a haze. The walls of the room we were standing in started closing in on me. I shook my head to clear it, but the haze was still there—for a wild moment I thought some of our Los Angeles smog had succeeded in tracking me down.

We were scheduled to do a show at Morón for several thousand Air Force men and their families. But I found myself in the base hospital, stretched out on an examining table between two young Air Force doctors.

The two young Air Force doctors examined me very thoroughly. The more thorough they were, the more worried I got. I know now what took them so long. They were used to working on strapping young air cadets, and my age bracket was a mystery to them.

They listened to my chest, poked, prodded, then ran up and down the scale a few times on my ribs.

I said, "Look, fellas, just tell me what's wrong and let me out of here. I've got a show to do."

While my mouth was open, they popped a knockout pill in it and parked my flab between the sheets.

While I slept in the base hospital, Hedda Hopper, Professor Colonna, Molly, Randy, Elaine, and Les Brown and the band put on the show. I awoke a couple of hours later feeling greatly refreshed. I felt so much better, I went over to the hangar where the performance was under way and walked out on the stage for the last part of the show. The audience didn't know anything was wrong. But I did. I knew that Mother Nature had given me a warning.

I feel I'm dwelling on the problems of a middle-aged comedian a little too long, and not telling you enough about the fun we all have on these tours. When you travel with a bunch of high-spirited people, you have a wonderful time. I've never met anyone yet who's made a USO tour who didn't look back on it as one of the high spots in his life.

For one thing, there's the good feeling you get from knowing that you're helping others. Then there's the zest of encountering new countries, new people, new places. You don't always have hot meals, or comfortable beds, or paved roads to travel over, and the other conveniences of our civilized world at home. But if you have even a spark of adventure in your makeup, you can overlook those things and have a whale of a time. I still laugh when I recall the way the various individuals in our group reacted to the circumstances we encountered overseas.

For instance, one ailment we couldn't take any shots for was "PX fever." All our overseas bases and installations have a store called the PX.

These stores carry a huge stock of all kinds of supplies to take care of the needs of the servicemen and their families. They not only carry the name-brand products we're all familiar with in stores here at home, but each PX also sells local wares of native manufacture. In Germany, you find fine German cameras in the PX; in Japan, jade and pearls and silk kimonos; in France, fine perfumes; and clean post cards.

As soon as our plane landed, there was always a rush for the PX. Our group bought cameras, binoculars, goatskin wine bottles, carved chess sets, music boxes—anything they could get their hands on. The guys in the band have a motto: If it doesn't move, buy it. If it moves, date it.

You could always tell when our group was visiting a base. The clerk of the PX would unlock the door in the morning and then run for his life. Our bunch in a PX makes Gimbels basement look like a rest camp.

To illustrate what I mean by "PX fever," one of our actors, Peter Leeds, spotted another member of our group carrying a package wrapped in brown paper. Without bothering to find out what was in the package, Pete rushed over to the PX clerk and said, "I'll take a dozen of those! What are they?"

And Pete wasn't the only one. Our engineer, John Pawlek, laid out two weeks' expense money for a Moroccan leather camel saddle. One of our cameramen brought back a string of Siamese temple bells. Our assistant engineer, a bachelor who lives in a small apartment, brought back a forty-by-forty Arabian prayer rug. That's the way the fever works. When you spot these "rare objects" in the PX, you've got to have it. Whether it's worth the price you have to pay for it, or whether you'll ever have any use at all for it never enters your mind. Our PX hounds gobbled up so much junk as the tour went on, our plane resembled a flying hockshop. Of course, I'm a much more experienced traveler, and the PX fever didn't hit me as hard as the others. I don't buy every little knickknack I see. By the way, if any of you are interested in buying a solid silver Egyptian goat-cheese mold, get in touch with me.

Only a few hours during the afternoon of December 20 had been allotted to our stop at Morón Air Base in Spain. The schedule for the rest of the day read, *"Fly to Madrid."* So I didn't have much time to worry about my physical condition; we were in the plane and on our way again.

Madrid was one of the high points of our tour. We were in a real city, billeted in a real hotel, the old but very elegant Castellana Hilton. Everyone who travels begins to wonder after a while how many hotels Conrad Hilton owns. I don't think even he knows from day to day what the total is, he has so many. You see the famous name in so many places, I can understand why someone chalked on one of the Egyptian pyramids, THE PHARAOH-HILTON.

One of the reasons we had included Madrid in our itinerary was to meet with Gina Lollobrigida, who was shooting a film there, and film a segment of my NBC television show with her.

I had planned this before leaving the States. I wanted to use Gina in a musical number in the TV show, so I cabled our agents in Spain, FIND OUT IF SHE CAN SING.

The reply arrived next morning. SHE SINGS AS WELL AS SHE ACTS. I stared at the brief words and wondered how to take them. This was either very high praise for Gina's vocalizing abilities, or the most cryptic message I had ever received.

I needn't have worried. When Gina opened her mouth, her first few notes set all my fears at rest. The Italian star is a very fine singer. But then, considering La Lollobrigida, I should've known her notes would be well-rounded, too!

I'd met Gina Lollobrigida briefly a few years before. Since that time, Gina had become world-famous. She was one of the handful of stars who had put Italy on the map, cinematically speaking.

I was looking forward to meeting her again, and I wasn't disappointed. I dropped in at her suite in the hotel. Gina, sheathed in white silk, glided up to me and husked throatily, "Hello, Bob."

At least I think that's what she said. I stood there enthralled as her dark lustrous eyes stared into mine, while her long eyelashes dusted the dandruff from my lapel. Gazing raptly at Gina's sultry loveliness, I suddenly knew why pizza had become Italy's second most popular dish.

Even her name is unusual and unique. Gina Lollobrigida! It sounds like a stick being run along a picket fence. But believe me, the resemblance ends there.

Like all actresses whose beauty is like a letter of credit at the bank, Gina was worried about how she would look on television. In the studio every shot is elaborately lighted, the angle is carefully considered, every shadow is just so. We were shooting in an aircraft hangar with the crudest of field equipment and hoping the cameramen could find the stage through the crowds. I consulted with Alan Stensvold, our genius cameraman, and told him I was worried.

He said, "Don't worry, Bob. She's a beautiful woman and we'll get it on film." And he did just that. He fiddled around with two lamps and a Zippo light and when we looked at the film, it was tremendous. I've seen Dave Forrest, our

How many actors work with a lookout? (*NBC photo*)

great sound man, do the same thing. People are tripping over the cords, the voltage is way off, the wind is stabbing the mikes. I look at Dave to see how it's going and he gives me the sign that it's fine. When we get back to the States, those little rolls of tape have got it all. I don't know how they do it. If I did, I could fire them both.

Gina was great on our TV show. We filmed a segment of the show at Torrejón, a nearby air base, and Gina was really a smash. She sang "Non Dimenticar" and although not many of our boys understood the Italian lyrics, as Gina stood there in the spotlight in a gold lamé sheath, they all got her message.

During our brief stop in Madrid, I was touted by the movie people into going to the El Duende Night Club to catch a terrific act, a group of flamenco dancers.

In Spain, flamenco dancers are about as rare as cornstalks in Kansas. But one glimpse of the El Duende flamenco dancers, and I was sold. They were so great, I stepped on the dance floor and hired them on the spot, to appear on my TV show.

Next morning, the flamenco dancers showed up, eager to do their act for our TV cameras. But there was one small detail I'd overlooked. Our cameras required a special voltage, and for that we needed a generator.

Finding a generator in Madrid makes the needle-in-a-haystack bit kid stuff. I commandeered a taxicab and spent a whole day scouring the city. I went to factories, stores, machine shops, used car lots—by the time I finally located a beat-up old generator, I'd been to more strange places than a contestant on "People Are Funny."

With a lot of pulling and hauling we got the generator aboard a rickety old truck. I gave the ancient Spaniard who was driving the truck explicit directions how to get to the studio where we would do the filming of the flamenco act. The Spanish truckman nodded to indicate he understood the directions, climbed in his truck and drove away, taking the generator with him. And we never saw him again. Where he drove to, or what happened to that generator, I never was able to find out.

So all our work and trouble went for nothing. The moral of this paragraph is: if you ever go to Madrid, bring your own generator.

In Madrid I ran into an old friend, our Ambassador to Spain, John Davis Lodge. Ambassador Lodge is a member of the distinguished Massachusetts family, but he hasn't let his blue blood lineage limit his activities. The last time I'd seen John Lodge was at Paramount twenty years before, when he was Marlene Dietrich's leading man in a picture called *The Scarlet Empress*.

Lodge shook my hand and said, "Bob, if you ever get tired of show business, we can use you. You'd make a great ambassador."

I said, "Me, an ambassador? What country are we that mad at?"

Although I passed it off with a corny attempt at a joke, underneath it gave me a warm feeling to have a man like John Davis Lodge think so highly of me. It wasn't till much later that the thought occurred to me that Mr. Lodge, too, is a man highly trained in diplomacy.

In conjunction with our stopover in Madrid, we'd planned to fly to Zaragoza Air Base, an hour or so away, and do a show for the Air Force.

But the bad weather suddenly clamped down again. Since Zaragoza was located in mountainous country, we decided to wait for the wind to die down.

After several hours of waiting, the plane carrying the band and our technical equipment took off into the teeth of the gale. Conditions at Zaragoza were even worse than at Madrid. The pilot made two attempts to land, then gave up and returned.

The weather remained bad all day, and I finally had to

call off the Zaragoza show. It was one of the few shows I've ever canceled.

Les Brown and his boys have flown with me all over the world and under all conditions. But when they stepped off the plane after those wild hours over Zaragoza, they were a mighty subdued bunch of musicians. Randy Sparks broke the tension and got quite a laugh when he said, "I wasn't scared, but I had visions of my wife being married to a much less talented singer!"

CHAPTER TEN

In the evening the weather cleared and we flew to our next scheduled stop, Naples.

It was only four hours by plane from Madrid to Naples . . . Or for you fellow stomach-travelers, the flight from Paella to Pizza was made in four Tums and a Bisodol. After two days of Spanish cooking, our plane wasn't the only thing that was tailheavy. We were to spend Christmas in Naples and our band of traveling locusts had practically stripped the PX at the airport. The plane's hold was so loaded with Christmas goodies, we didn't know till we landed that we had shanghaied the sergeant in charge of loading. He got wedged between a case of castanets and a pearl-handled garlic press and couldn't get out. The flight itself was not a memorable one except for a remark by one of my writers, who shall be nameless, and who should be jobless. Hedda Hopper, during one of the plane's unscheduled dips, had plaintively asked, "Aren't we going to have a Christmas tree like we did last year?" And before I could reply, "Snarling Charlie" rasped, "If we fly a little lower, we may."

Later at the Vesuvio Hotel in Naples, I sought to impress him by remarking, "Did you know that Caruso died in this hotel?" Only to have him snap back with, "I didn't even know he played here." . . . a truly wonderful line which I was to ad-lib some months later at a B'nai B'rith banquet.

I was in pajamas, brushing my teeth, when I glanced out at the bay and saw a sight I'll never forget. It was two days before Christmas, and half a dozen ships of our Sixth Fleet were in port for the Christmas holidays. These ships were anchored in a row across the bay and were festooned with long strings of Christmas lights from crow's nest to water-line. This spectacle of our ships ablaze with necklaces of colored Christmas lights all across the Bay of Naples tops everything in my memory.

Among the ships in the bay was our gigantic aircraft carrier, the *Forrestal*. We were scheduled to do an open-air show on its deck for the six thousand sailors of its crew.

But the next morning the dark clouds were on the job again. The skies opened up and it poured. The heavenly blessedness came down all day long, a steady, drenching downpour. By evening there wasn't a dry pizza in all Naples.

Of course, the storm knocked off our open-air show. We decided to postpone until the following afternoon.

Our gang grabbed the opportunity to do a little sightseeing and shopping in the rain.

The musicians took the trip out to Mount Vesuvius and were properly impressed. The trombone player stared at the smoking crater and said, "Dig that crazy ashtray!"

I don't think our musicians were sufficiently grounded in the glories of ancient history to appreciate Italy. At Pompeii they stared out over the magnificent ruins, then Les Brown said in awed tones, "Man, what a party!"

I was stuck with a whole afternoon of inactivity and the lull was getting me down, so I decided to walk around the town a bit and pick up a few trinkets to send home. I got more than I bargained for. I hadn't taken more than ten steps from the hotel when one of the strolling sidewalk merchants had offered to sell me, in rapid succession, a Parker pen, a diamond wristwatch, an original drawing by Michelangelo with calendar attached, a case of Scotch-type whiskey and eight jeep hub caps. The prices he quoted were so fantastically low, only a sucker would lose sight of the fact that the merchandise was probably phony. I got rid of him in a hurry. Lucky I did, too. Later, when I tried to write with the pen, it came apart in my hand, and the wrist-watch stopped running long before the peddler did. I'm glad I didn't go for the Michelangelo original; it was probably stolen.

The next day, the skies cleared and we went aboard the *Forrestal*. The Commanding Officer, Captain Allen Shinn, took me on a tour of the carrier. I didn't realize what I'd let myself in for. Below decks, there's miles and miles of corridors. Before we'd finished half the inspection, I was wishing I'd brought along my golfmobile. From bow to stern of the *Forrestal* is a sleeper jump. It's so enormous, the captain still hasn't seen all of it himself. To give you an idea of the size of the ship, one young sailor was lost for several days, wandering around below decks. They found him when he walked up to a bos'n's mate and said, "Pardon me, sir, could you direct me to the ocean?"

The vast expanse of deck was an awesome sight to our pop-eyed group. Barbara Fishel, our script girl, ventured to the edge where there was no rail, just a sheer drop to the water. "How do you keep from falling off?" she asked a sailor. "We don't," came the reply. "This is the only ship in the Navy with a shark escort."

We set up our cameras on the flight deck of the *Forrestal* and went ahead with preparations for our show. As we worked, I was conscious of our old friends, the dark clouds, gathering overhead. The wind was blowing in gusts, and there were whitecaps all around us on the bay. But we continued stringing cables and setting up lights, and hoped for the best.

By show time, a huge audience of sailors covered the deck of the *Forrestal*. They hung in the rigging, on the radar masts, every point from which our stage could be seen.

The bay was so choppy now, even the *Forrestal* was rocking slightly. The rising wind made eerie whistling noises in our microphones. Our engineers solved this by borrowing some wool socks and pulling them over the mikes.

As the skies darkened, it became apparent we might not be able to finish our show before another storm struck. I was in a quandary what to do. In our tight schedule, no allowance had been made for bad weather. We'd already delayed one day, and another delay was out of the question. Waiting for a clear day in the Bay of Naples in December is like waiting for the smog to lift in Los Angeles. I looked at the expectant faces of the sailors surrounding us, and the decision was made for me. On with the show.

Despite the wind and an occasional shower of spray, our show was going along fine. The sailors were an enthusiastic audience. Just when I began to think we might fool the weatherman after all, the deluge struck, and with no gentle pitter-patter; that rain hit the deck of the *Forrestal* with a roar. In a second, players and audience alike were soaked to the skin. In those falling sheets of water, there was no question of continuing on with the show. Even Lloyd Bridges would've called it a day.

But I'd reckoned without the Navy. Those sailors grabbed the stage, cameras, equipment, everything that was portable, and lugged them to the huge plane elevator. I could hardly believe my eyes as the elevator sank slowly, carrying the whole show setup to the deck below. Shielded from the rain, the sailors of the *Forrestal* reassembled our entire show just as it had been on the deck above. An hour later, we continued with the performance. Mark Twain said everyone talks about the weather but nobody does anything about it. Well, my friends on the *Forrestal* crossed up the Connecticut sage. When the weather interfered with their fun, they did something about it!

Our platoon of journalists was having a fine time on the tour. Distinguished-looking John Reddy of *Reader's Digest* and Eleanor Harris of *McCall's* turned out to be dyed-in-the-wool tourists. They, with Barney McNulty, our sign man, would get up at 5 A.M. and rush off in all directions to visit art galleries, museums, and all points of interest in every country we visited. The rest of us wanted to see the sights, too, but we didn't have the strength of character of this hopped-up trio. Somehow, at 5 A.M. of a rainy morning in Madrid, the Sealy looked better to me than anything El Greco ever painted. Although I've never slept on an El Greco. While I love the excitement of visiting other countries, I'm not one to claw my way up to the Matterhorn just for the privilege of yelling "Excelsior!" when I get to the top. When I want to see the scenic points, I go over to the lobby newsstand and whirl the post card rack.

Hedda Hopper, of course, was all over the place. Hedda's a great mixer, as much at home at a rocket base as she is at Romanoff's.

As we waited in the wings to go onstage for our show at Torrejón, Hedda turned to me and said, "What am I doing here, Bob? I gave up one-night stands thirty years ago!"

I said, "You're here for the same reason I am, Hedda. You're a big ham!"

Which is about as close to a compliment as people in show business toss at one another. I knew Hedda wasn't climbing in and out of planes and slopping across muddy airfields day and night just for the thrill of hearing a little applause.

I'd had my writers dream up a few jokes that Hedda could tell during her stint onstage, but I don't believe Hedda ever got to them. When I introduced Hedda, she breezed out, grabbed the microphone and said, "All right, fellows, just throw some questions at me about Hollywood, and I'll do my best to answer them." That was her act, and the way Hedda answered the questions was a caution. A lot of her answers would never get by in Boston.

At Port Lyautey, one sailor in the audience asked, "What's new on Brigitte Bardot?" Without a second's hesitation, Hedda answered, "*Anything* on Brigitte Bardot is new!"

After I heard that answer, I didn't worry about Hedda's ability to take care of herself on the stage. I just made a

On the flight deck of the USS Forrestal. *Just before the rains came.*
(*NBC photo*)

mental reservation not to get in any public ad-libbing sessions with her!

On Christmas Eve our little band of gypsies gathered in the dining room of our hotel in Naples and had dinner together. We all felt a little emotional. There's something about Christmas Eve that makes you feel very conscious of every mile of the distance you're away from home and loved ones.

At first we were all pretty subdued, like sheep huddled together for shelter, but after a glass of vino we perked up enough to sing "Deck the Halls" and "Silent Night."

179

I noticed that Professor Colonna, sitting next to me, was served a different dish from the rest of us. The chef carried in and set in front of the Mad Stash a huge steaming casserole. It looked delicious, and it easily out-aromaed our plates of spaghetti. I said, "What's that?"

"Pasta fagioli," the Stash informed me, his fork never losing its rhythm as it traveled back and forth, tucking huge portions under his beaver.

"Great," I said, "where's mine?"

It developed there was no *pasta fagioli* for any of the rest of us. We were in Italy, where Colonna ranks in importance with our Presidents. Being of Italian descent, the Professor is the hero of the boot country. From Palermo to Parma, from Turin to Rome, the Stash ranks with such Italian greats as Caesar, Caruso, Perry Como, Dean Martin, and Sinatra. In the land of ravioli and the meatball, the Professor outranked all of us.

But Jerry's not one to rub it in. He graciously passed out snacks of his *pasta fagioli* to the rest of us, after he'd eaten all he could put away himself.

Caruso, we were told in Italy, once shattered a champagne glass with a high note. A GI in the audience during our show in Naples called out and asked Colonna if he could do this. "No," the Professor replied, "but I once made a bowl of goldfish mighty nervous!"

As is our custom on Christmas Eve, most of the cast went to midnight Mass at the huge cathedral, one of the most beautiful in Europe.

The next day, we hopped to Vicenza and put on a Christmas show for the men stationed at our rocket base there. On a long tour with a great many stops, such as this one, you find yourself climbing in and out of the plane every day, and you begin to take the flying for granted. You stop worrying about whether you'll get there safely or not; it becomes as commonplace as taking the bus to work every day.

Our planes, pilots, and crews functioned so perfectly, we just didn't expect any mishaps. But in Vicenza we had a close call. For a great many of us on the tour, it came close to being our last Christmas on earth.

While our show was going on, our two planes were being refueled so that we could take off later in the day for Frankfurt, Germany.

The planes were ready for us when we returned. The musicians and several members of our cast were boarding the first plane when Captain Coddington came along. And at this moment, the alertness of this officer saved a great many lives. The captain sniffed the air, still laden with the fumes of the fuel which had been put in the plane's tanks, and the alarm bell rang in his mind. It wasn't the right smell for the fuel that our planes required.

The captain immediately had the plane cleared and the fuel pumped out. By mistake, the plane had been loaded with a type fuel used by the jet fighters stationed at the base. Had that plane managed to take off, it might have exploded in mid-air and, as they say, "What would we have done for an encore?"

With the right fuel in our tanks, we took off from Vicenza and flew north toward Germany. I guess the incident at Vicenza had made me a little nervous. I went up to the pilot's cabin to check on things. We were crossing the jagged, snow-covered peaks of the Alps, and after our experience of an hour before, those peaks looked very sharp and menacing as they passed a few hundred feet below our wings.

Our pilot told me there was a more direct route to our destination, Frankfurt, but we were following the "corridor."

The cold war with Russia was at its chilliest at the time; if our plane strayed out of the corridor, there was a good chance of our being forced down by Russian Migs, several of which we could see in the distance. Wandering out of that air corridor was more risky than changing lanes on the freeway.

Whenever I appear before Air Force men, I usually do a routine about how calm I am when I'm flying. One of my jokes goes, "Flying over to Europe I read a novel. Coming back I read the second page."

After the incident at Vicenza, that's the way I felt that afternoon as I stared down at those sharp mountain peaks and then over at those Russian fighter planes. I was so nervous, I started to bite my fingernails, but I discovered I'd already finished them.

Luckily, our pilot stuck to the safety corridor with the doggedness of a New Year's reveler following the white line on his way home in a fog. Every once in a while a Mig would come close and take a look at us, but aside from this game of aerial peekaboo, nothing happened. We finally left the Alps behind and headed down into the Rhein-Main Air Base at Frankfurt, Germany.

A big party had been arranged for us at the home of Lieutenant General F. W. Farrell, Chief of the Berlin Command. The general had a lovely home in Frankfurt. We walked in to find the general and his wife waiting for us, and a very elegant and elaborate buffet dinner in a huge room illuminated by candlelight.

This warm and gracious reception took our little band of international beatniks completely by surprise. We had suddenly stepped back into civilization and we loved it.

Donn Trenner, Les Brown's piano player, was staggered by the presence of five or six generals. It looked like our All-Star team had been called off the bench. Donn, who had been a buck private in the Army, admitted to the wife of one of the generals that all that brass around made him so nervous, he had a powerful urge to leave and go home. "I wish," replied the wife, "the Russians felt that way so I could go home!"

After our struggles with the bad weather in Italy, putting

on shows under adverse conditions, and hopping around like a flea on a hot stove, the lovely surroundings, good food and drink, and the graciousness of our hosts really got to me. I relaxed. And it proved to be my undoing. I hadn't known it, but since Spain I'd been going along on nerve alone.

I don't exactly know what happened, but one moment I was chatting with a group of people, and the next someone was grabbing my arm and saying, "What's the matter, Bob, you look sick."

And I was hardly in any position to deny it. I'd tottered over to a chair and was sprawled in it, watching the room and the people swirl by like the horses on a merry-go-round.

Several people grabbed me and assisted me upstairs to the general's bed. I could hardly believe it—I had collapsed. I was laid out like a sturgeon in Barney Greengrass's window.

As I was helped into the general's bedroom, I felt terrible. I'd violated the comedian's basic rule: I'd left an audience without an exit line.

My previous malaise in Morón, Spain, hadn't caused much of a stir. Only a few people of our group had known about it. But this time it was different. I'd picked an almost-public place for my latest swan dive. It's hard to conk out gracefully and without attracting any attention in a roomful of people.

As helping hands assisted me up the stairway, I could hear one of my press people, Ursula Halloran, saying, "Don't get excited, folks, it's nothing."

But Ursula had reckoned without our contingent of newspaper reporters who'd been waiting all during the tour for any kind of a news break. Ursula tried to prevent them from climbing up the stairway. She didn't succeed. A flying wedge shoved past her. Atra Baer said, "Get out of the way, honey, and let the pros take over!"

Within ten minutes, every phone in the neighborhood had been commandeered by the members of our press contingent. By next morning, my collapse would be read about at breakfast tables from Maine to Mombasa.

Lying there in the general's bed, I was both sick and extremely surprised. Two hours before, I had entered Germany a comedian. And here I was, a party-pooper.

The whole experience was very embarrassing. I've been written up in dozens of articles and newspaper stories as Mr. Perpetual Motion, Mr. Energy, the tireless traveler and globetrotter; and here I was, flatter than a bride's first cake, etched on the percale like a pressed flower in an old maid's diary.

I vetoed the idea of checking into a hospital for a few days' rest. After a night's sleep, I awoke feeling refreshed and fairly normal. I felt so well, in fact, I enjoyed the story of my collapse in the local paper.

That afternoon we put on a show for the men stationed at the Rhein-Main Air Base near Frankfurt. The men gave me an ovation as I walked out on the stage. I said, "I'm very happy to be here—and I mean that!"

And, needless to say, I really did mean it. Everything looked very, very good to me that day—the sunshine, the trees rustling in the breeze, even a sign on a German butcher shop advertising a sale of pig's liver was a thing of beauty.

After the show at Rhein-Main, we climbed back into our DC-6s and flew to Berlin. We were back on schedule and it was just another workday.

Everyone on the plane seemed very solicitous of my comfort. Colonel Layden, our liaison officer, brought me a cup of hot cocoa, then dropped into the seat next to me and told me some great war anecdotes. Here's one I especially liked.

It happened when President Eisenhower was Commander-in-Chief of the allied forces. After the Normandy landing on D-Day, Ike came ashore soaked to the skin. He had a raincoat thrown over his shoulders which covered his insignia. He stopped at a supply truck and requested a pair of shoes to replace his wet ones. The supply sergeant said, "What size?" Ike couldn't remember his exact size, and the supply sergeant mumbled, "You oughta know your own shoe size, buddy!" Just then the raincoat slipped off Ike's shoulder, revealing the row of stars. The dumfounded supply sergeant said, "Well I'll be a — — — —! The Milky Way!"

As the colonel and I sat swapping stories in the plane, a jet aircraft buzzed past our window. I asked the colonel what type of aircraft it was, and he said, "Don't worry about it, Bob . . . if you can see it, it's obsolete."

Flying into Berlin is quite a trick in itself. Tempelhof Air Base is located smack in the center of a thickly populated suburb. It's surrounded on all sides by apartment buildings.

As we circled over these structures, I asked our pilot, "How do you find your way in?"

He said, "It's a cinch, Bob. I just follow the clotheslines right down the runway."

And he wasn't kidding. It's sort of a drip-dry landing. I kept my fingers crossed as we swooped down between the tall buildings. Through many of the windows, we could see families eating dinner.

We drove to the brand-new, ultramodern Berlin Hilton Hotel. We arrived at the height of the dinner hour and trudged in through the throngs of fashionably dressed people in the lobby, looking like a long-lost Major Bowes unit. The Berlin Hilton had opened just a few days before, and it wasn't really organized yet. I'm sure the house detective would've thrown us all out if he'd had a little more confidence.

West Germany is thriving in the midst of a fabulous business boom, which is one of the reasons the Russians so urgently want us out of Berlin. The contrast between the plenty that is available under the democratically occupied section of Germany and the squalor in the Eastern Zone is a pretty bad selling point for Communism.

When we checked into the hotel, what amazed us most were the flocks of sightseers window-shopping among the stores and shops in the hotel arcade. It was like date night at Disneyland. People were four and five deep, trying to get a peek in the windows, and this went on all day long.

The hotel is extremely modern, with some innovations which I have not yet seen in American hotels. The room phone, for example, has lights on it to indicate that you have had a call in your absence.

I was impressed by the glitter of the place. The motif of the interior decorating seemed to be lions, giraffes, and tigers. The desk clerk explained, "The zoo is right next door." Then he added, "It was once the greatest zoo in the world. But no more. During the war we ate all the animals."

When I got to my room, the phone was ringing. It was Dolores, calling from North Hollywood. Her first words were, "Are you all right, Bob?"

I told her I was fine. Dolores sounded a little frantic; she'd been trying to reach me for twenty-four hours. I told her I felt great, never better in my life, that my seizure had only been a temporary thing and I was absolutely in the pink. When I finished, Dolores said, "That's fine. Now stop lying to me and put your doctor on the phone!"

That's what I love about Dolores. Everything I tell her she believes implicitly, and she keeps on believing it until she can check up and find out the truth. Dolores is one-third Irish, one-third Italian, and one-third lie detector.

We did our show that evening in the Fluegelhorst Gymnasium in Berlin. All servicemen in the area were off duty for the holidays, and the building was packed.

At this particular time, Russia was putting on great pressure to get us out of West Berlin, but the West Berliners were standing firm. A banner across the stage read, *BERLIN, THE OUTPOST OF DEMOCRACY!*

And that's exactly the way our audience felt. They responded to everything we said with tremendous enthusiasm, and our jokes about the Russians got roars of approval. It was one of the greatest audiences I've ever played to.

After every show, there's always several GIs who come up to say hello to me, or shake hands, or who want to tell about having seen me at some other base or camp. This has been going on for years, and has become more or less routine, but here at Fluegelhorst, one very young-looking GI pulled a new one on me.

As this youthful GI shook my hand, he said, "My father told me if I ever met you to say 'hello.'"

I said, "Oh, that's wonderful. Who's your father?"

He replied, "Oh, you don't know him, but you played for him in 1944 on Guadalcanal."

I entertained his father! That one line really aged me. Numbly I said, "I hope your grandfather caught me at Appomattox. I was really a smash there!"

During our stay in Berlin, several members of our group went sightseeing over into East Berlin, in the Russian Sector. Our press agent, Frank Liberman, tried to strike up a conversation with a soldier standing guard at the Russian war memorial.

Frank walked up and said, "Hello, Ivan!"

The Russian soldier at first stared impassively, then gave a grudging nod.

But Frank knew how to break the ice. He held out a five-dollar bill and pointed at the hammer-and-sickle insignia on the collar of the Russian's tunic. He indicated by sign language that he wanted to trade.

The Russian looked around cautiously, then took the money. Then he removed the Soviet emblem from his uniform and handed it over.

There's no punch-line to this incident, except that the next time you watch an NBC show in which someone wears a Russian uniform, you can be sure the insignia is authentic.

The network uses the insignia Frank bought from "Ivan" that day in East Berlin.

After the show at the Fluegelhorst Gymnasium, Hedda Hopper and I stopped in at the Resi Bar, a nightclub that is one of the tourist attractions of Berlin. The Resi is a combined dance hall, beerstube, and trysting place, sort of a Lonely Hearts Club with pretzels. Resi is pronounced "racy" and it fits; lonely visiting firemen can always find feminine companionship there, via a very unusual gimmick. The booths and tables are connected by phones. You just look around, pick out someone who takes your fancy, and dial the other person's booth number. It's sort of Bingo with girls.

I was sitting with Hedda surveying the scene when the phone on our table rang. I picked it up and a sultry voice said, "Bob? Welcome to Berlin."

It was a pretty little *Fräulein* a few booths away, and she wanted our autographs. While we had dinner, our phone rang several times. One young GI came over to our table and asked, "When's Bing coming to Berlin?" I told him, "Since Bing got married, we not only can't get him to Berlin, we can't get him out of the house!"

An American couple said, "We're also staying at the Hilton, Bob, how come we never see you around the hotel?"

I explained that on tour my hotel room is my work headquarters. My usual routine is to have breakfast in my room and then sit around with my writers beating out a few up-to-the-minute jokes for the show we're going to do that evening. We look through the local newspapers for hot, current topics and items of local interest. I have a great love for the topical joke, the political joke. I like to mention names in the news, I like to spear a topic while it's hot.

Sometimes a member of the troupe will ad-lib a line we can use in the show. Les Brown, after hiking the length of the deck of the immense carrier *Forrestal* said, "Whew! Now I know why they call it a 'poop deck!'"

In Berlin, we were all impressed when our plane dropped down between tall apartment buildings. That, together with the Russian fighter planes patrolling the air corridor, made for an extremely ticklish situation.

Discussing it in our hotel room huddle, I started a chain reaction with, "Flying here is really dangerous. This is the only place in the world where the pigeons travel by bus." I was topped immediately by Charlie Lee who riposted, "Sometimes the Russian fighters come alongside to look you over. You hope they're just window-shopping." Les White parlayed that into an applause-grabber with "What a nerve test! It's like sitting in a cellophane chair with a broken bottle underneath!" And so it went. Mort Lachman picked up the ball with a few barbs I could aim at myself. For example: "You know, there's quite a tense situation here. The Russians want to take over West Berlin. Of course, that was before I arrived." Johnny Rapp chimed in with, "The Russians will never take over the Berlin Hilton. Not at those prices." Bill Larkin expanded, "The first six floors are reserved for International Spies. The house detective is Peter Lorre." The session finally ended with, "I'm happy to say that the people over here really know me. Whenever I walk down the street here in West Berlin, everybody follows me yelling and cheering. Tell me, what does '*Schweine-hund*' mean?" I don't know whose joke that was, but I'm sure he's no longer with me.

We stayed in West Berlin for three days, and it was kind of an eerie feeling spending Christmas there. On my lone sojourn into the Eastern Sector I had my pass okayed by an armed Santa Claus. It was quiet there and I had the feeling that they'd like to put up a Christmas tree, too, if there were any trees left to put up.

Our trip was on its last leg and from the way I'd been feeling, we were about even . . . All that remained was Keflavik and Goose Bay; after that it was home, orange blossoms, and a two-week layoff to recharge my batteries.

I was looking forward to our short stopover at Prestwick, Scotland, because I knew that while they were refueling I'd have almost two hours to browse among the kilts and tartans in the local PX. I should have known better. The moment we touched down, I had my choice of lunch or an audience of a couple of hundred servicemen and their families. They probably would have boiled my steak anyway.

The CO had told us that a group of Air Force wives and children were watching a movie nearby, so we went over. The projectionist stopped the film and I got up on the stage and ran through a few of my routines. Then I made a mistake. I said, "Does anyone have any questions?"

A little kid sitting in the front row piped up. "Yeah. When are they gonna put the movie back on?"

An hour later we were in the air again, headed for Iceland. At Prestwick, we had picked up a civilian who was going our way to Keflavik. The five-hour trip was the roughest of our entire journey. Our civilian passenger, a stranger to us all, picked a particularly rough spot to get up and walk around. "Who's that?" said Elaine Dunne, "I've never seen him before."

"I don't know," replied Hedda, "I just hope it's not Mr. Jordan."

Our second plane, I learned later, had to return to Prestwick to pick up a left-behind member of the band, the drummer, who had dallied too long in the snack bar. Not only that, after the plane was in the air again, the drummer recalled he'd been having some liquid refreshment with the saxophone player, who had excused himself from the table for a few minutes. A check of the plane revealed the sax player was not among those present. So the plane had to turn around again and go back and make a second landing.

The sax player was standing at the edge of the airstrip, waiting. He said, "Man, I was afraid you cats would *never* come back!" The reason he was afraid was he was a bourbon drinker and he didn't want to be stuck in Scotland.

Before the plane took off again, the pilot insisted that a nose-count be made. Les Brown said, "That won't be necessary. Fellows, get out your instruments and strike a chord—I'll know if anyone's missing!"

It was dark when we landed in Keflavik, Iceland. An Air Force band was drawn up beside the runway, playing "Thanks for the Memory" in the icy wind.

I said to an officer, "Please, get those guys out of the cold!"

He said, "Shhh! It would break their hearts—they've been practicing all week!"

I still can't get over the sight of that wonderful, frostbitten GI band standing in a gale and blowing my theme song at 4 above zero. I found out later it took a crew of medics to separate the trumpet player's lips from his horn. And people ask me why we make these trips!

I figured the least we could do under the circumstances was hear them out, so we all stood there, getting more numb by the minute, till the end of the rendition. Then we all rushed for the hot coffee.

Keflavik is not one of the favorite posts of our GIs overseas, to put it mildy. We'd kept this in mind when we prepared our material for the show. At that time, the rotation system was their biggest gripe. I threw in a line, "At night it's very quiet here. All you can hear is the wind blowing through the trees, and the sobbing of a sergeant who doesn't have enough points to get out!"

Those GIs at Keflavik were really homesick, and it wasn't hard to tell what they missed most. When Molly Bee and Elaine Dunne came out on the stage, the boys raised the roof.

At 3 A.M. we were back in our planes and a few minutes later we were headed out over the North Atlantic toward the last stop before home—Goose Bay, Labrador. I immediately fell fast asleep in my plane seat.

I was having a terrific dream in which I was just leaving

the stage of the Academy Awards presentations with my arms full of Oscars when I felt a tug at my shoulder. Our pilot, Captain Ray Coddington, was shaking me.

He said, "Excuse me, Bob, but we're going over some weather stations and I thought you'd like to say hello to the men."

I staggered up the aisle to the captain's cabin. The plane was dim, everyone sprawled in their seats snoring away, sort of a flying Sealy.

Someone handed me a microphone and, standing behind the captain's seat, I was on. It was an eerie sensation, talking by radio to the weather-station boys somewhere below us in the dark.

The first voice that came through identified himself as an officer of the Ocean Station Bravo, a weather ship. He said, "How you doing up there, Bob? Sorry we couldn't get to see any of your shows."

I said, "Man, you guys stationed out here away from the traffic have really got it made. How'd you guys get the job —politics?"

To my surprise, the voice crackled back, "They had to give us the job—we own the thermometer!"

Imagine getting caught in an ad-lib session at four in the morning twenty thousand feet over the North Atlantic, and being topped by a guy you can't even see? I said, "I'll write to Washington and have your option picked up for another four years. This kind of competition I don't need!"

They told us the whole crew of the weather ship was out of their bunks and gathered around the radio listening, so I went into a few of my routines for them. I'll never know what kind of laughs I got, if any, but it was a show I loved doing. We swapped stories, small talk, the football scores, etc.

We woke up Jerry Colonna, Molly Bee, and Randy Sparks and they got into the act. Colonna sang his crazy version of "Mandalay" for them, Randy did a few numbers, and

Molly Bee sang and talked with a couple of southern boys in the weather ship crew. Our radio that night was the jumpingest party line in the North Atlantic.

As Ocean Station Bravo faded out of our range, the Coast Guard weather ship *McCullough* came in. With a new audience, we stayed on our radio mike and repeated our little show all over again. We also talked to a station on the Pinetree early warning radar line.

Molly Bee talked to one southern boy from Bell Buckle, Tennessee. After singing a song for him, Molly asked the boy what else he'd like to hear. His voice came back, "Just keep talking, ma'am!"

I had to hand it to our little group for giving up their holiday and a chance to be with their families at home. I know they were repaid for the hardships they endured, in the knowledge that they were entertaining a lot of kids who couldn't get home for the holidays either.

At dawn we landed in Goose Bay, Labrador. We were to stay in Goose Bay only long enough to refuel, so we hurried through breakfast and rushed into the washrooms for a freshening-up. The men were lined up in front of the wash basins for a much-needed shave, and just as we got lathered up, the lights went out. It was a temporary power failure. There isn't much you can do with a faceful of hot lather except shave it off, so we all went ahead anyway, in the pitch dark. There was a lot of joking and grunting, and occasionally you'd get hit by a gob of wet lather flipped at what someone thought was the sink. The whole thing was like a Gillette commercial in a coal mine.

The lights came on again just in time—Professor Colonna had accidentally trimmed off a hunk of his mustache. One side of his upper lip was almost clean-shaven, which produced a very weird effect. The Professor looked like his mustache was signaling a left turn. He looked like a beatnik who couldn't make up his mind.

At Goose Bay we said good-bye to our wonderful MATS

crews, who had piloted our two planes safely for over fourteen thousand miles.

As these guys walked out to their planes to fly back to their home base near Washington, we all lined up and gave them an enthusiastic round of applause. And that applause came from our hearts.

As I shook hands with Captain Coddington, I said, "I wish I could steal you away from the Air Force. Have you ever thought of going into show business?"

Looking me in the eye, he came back with, "No thanks—it's too risky!"

CHAPTER ELEVEN

I am not really a coward. My psychiatrist explained the whole thing to me. It is normal for a man to respect danger, and when it comes to danger, believe me, I'm as normal as you can get.

In 1960, when Khrushchev's illegitimate son, the Cuban beatnik, moved into the Havana Hilton without registering, I didn't even have to look at our orders from the Defense Department. The Bob Hope troupe was committed to a seven-day tour of the Caribbean bases, ending on Christmas Day at the hot spot: Guantánamo Bay.

I had a right to be nervous. Not only did I have my own skin to worry about, but where was I going to find stars who were not only willing to give up their holidays at home but were anxious to perform in a target area?

Fortunately, Hollywood is loaded with kooks. When we assembled at NBC for our first trip briefing, I couldn't believe the list of stars who turned up for roll call. What a lineup: Andy Williams, the world's only non-Italian singer; Anita Bryant, the hottest thing on records; Delores Gay, a stunning dancer who broke a nightclub date in Chicago and flew out to make the gig; my co-star in *Bachelor in Paradise*, Janis Paige, who left a movie contract and a fiancé to join us; and a shy, unassuming miss with the improbable name of Zsa Zsa Gabor, star of stage, screen, and marriages. And just to fill out the roster, we had our old faithfuls Professor Colonna and the Les Brown Band who welcomed the danger. They'll do anything for an excuse to drink.

In charge of the briefing was our favorite project officer,

Major Ed Swinney. Big Ed has taken us all over the world, and I'm afraid our troupe has been something of a shock treatment for him. Today he is the show's biggest fan. When first we met, he looked upon us as a raggle-taggle bunch of 4-Fs who would have to be whipped into shape. Everything was going to be by the numbers. He planned on reveille at six, followed by calisthenics.

There was nothing in the Air Force Manual that could possibly have prepared him for his first skirmish with Zsa Zsa. I don't have a tape of the conversation. If I did, I know it would make a best-selling album.

For openers, the major walked over to Zsa Zsa and said, "Miss Gabor, I would like to ask you a few questions." Zsa Zsa instantly replied, "It wouldn't do you any good, darlink, I can tell you're a married man." There was a nervous silence, broken only by the rattling of the major's oak leaf clusters.

The major decided on a more oblique attack. "Miss Gabor, I noticed that you haven't had your shots yet."

"No thank you, darlink—I don't drink in the morning."

"No, no, Miss Gabor, inoculations. Shots for the prevention of disease; the Air Force requires it."

Zsa Zsa laughed at the stupidity of it all. "Shots are for Americans, they're such clean people. We Europeans eat a lot of dirt, we don't catch no diseases. You can have mine."

And you know, the major took them. About that time he needed a shot.

Monday morning, December nineteenth, as the early rays of the sun fought their way through the smog hanging over Burbank airport, 59 vagrants, still shivering from their yellow fever shots, climbed aboard our MATS Constellation.

It was to be a tight little trip. We were scheduled to do fifteen shows in seven days. That's the Defense Department for you, they give you nineteen shots and don't give you time to catch anything.

Peter Leeds, Prof. Colonna, Andy Williams, Zsa Zsa, Anita Bryant, Old Sincere, Janis Paige, Delores Gay, and Les Brown. The Trapp family at the Guantánamo Hilton. (NBC photo)

Our first play-date, Panama, was 4500 miles away. We made one quick stop at Mobile, Alabama, where we picked up gas for the plane and changed the alcohol in Colonna's jar.

From there it was eleven hours to Panama, and that's a long time on a plane. I started flying with the Air Force back when they only had bucket seats. Now that I've got the body for it, they've changed the equipment. After a jet, those prop-jobs have a lot of Stepin Fetchit going for them.

To while away the hours on our airborne buckboard, we played games like "Twenty Questions." The idea was to ask Zsa Zsa twenty questions without getting your face slapped. I lost.

Panama is a very small country, but we're lucky it's there. Otherwise, the Pacific Ocean would leak all over the Atlantic. The Canal Zone itself is the weirdest piece of property over which the Stars and Stripes wave. It is a strip of land about ten miles wide, rented to Uncle Sam. It's one of our most strategic areas and we have 10,000 men down there making sure nobody pulls the stopper.

Geographically speaking, Panama is in the Torrid Zone. And they're not kidding. When we stepped off the plane at Albrook Air Force Base at Balboa, we were hit by a blast of hot, moist air. We weren't sure whether we landed on an airstrip, a car wash, or the Big Ditch itself.

We could hardly wait to get to our quarters at Fort Clayton to take a shower. But it wasn't any use, by the time you got out of the shower your clothes were sticking to you again. It's no place for a girl with anything to hide.

Every closet is equipped with a dehumidifier. You have to keep all your clothes and your shoes in it at night, otherwise you'll wake up in the morning with a sneaker full of penicillin.

The sheets on the bed were wringing wet. It's awful when even your bed isn't housebroken. We used to pour a half-inch of talcum powder on the sheets and try to fall asleep before the damp seeped through. In the morning we'd get up, our bodies caked with powder, looking like breaded zombies.

We really had to hustle to make our schedule. In quick succession we played Albrook, Fort Clayton, then hopped across the moat to Fort Kobbe, where one of the nightmares happened.

We were doing a far-out piece in which Colonna was an Army Engineer in charge of the canal locks. It built to a big

A white Xmas with the Navy in Panama. (NBC photo)

finish in which Colonna closed the gate in front of the air-craft carrier *Forrestal*. There was to be a huge crash and then, as the *Forrestal* sank, Colonna would say, "What do you know, we now have the biggest gol-darn submarine in the world!"

Everything went fine, Jerry got a lot of laughs on the build-up, but when it came time for the big crash, there was silence. We waited and waited, there was still complete silence. I was on camera and couldn't turn away, but out of the corner of my eye, I saw our prop man, Al Borden, and it was a sight I'll never forget.

Normally, in a studio, three men would be handling a crash sound effect of this size. Al had to do it alone. In his left hand he had a boat whistle attached to a cylinder of compressed air; in his right hand, some chains with which to beat on some sheet metal; his foot was tied to a door with a creaking hinge for the gate effect; his mouth was over a straw in a glass of water to make the bubbling, sinking sound. When the cue came, Al froze; he just couldn't figure out which part to move first. I couldn't help it, I broke up and ruined the whole hunk of film.

Al Borden has probably given me more laughs, intentionally and otherwise, than anyone else in the business. We first worked together when he was a property man back on Broadway and he's been with me ever since I've been in television. In fact, Al probably has more time on camera than I have. He has an innate knack for finding his way in front of a live camera. He has all the grace and agility of Smokey the Bear. If he doesn't stumble in front of the camera, he's bound to fall off a ladder into the middle of a love scene. I don't know why he isn't listed in *TV Guide*. He's the only prop man in the business that wears make-up.

Al does all the wild effects you see on our show. For one sketch, he built a vacuum cleaner that maneuvered around the room by itself. In a golf sketch with Sam Snead, he rigged a ball that danced all over the green before dropping in the cup. For a song of Wally Cox, he made a trick beer stein. Wally would blow the foam off, and it would swoop back on the glass.

However, with Al—not everything is guaranteed. Once he was to lower a champagne bucket gently into a scene; he bounced it neatly off my skull.

Once we flew him all the way to Casablanca to handle the props on a TV show. When we got to Morocco, we discovered Al had left the prop trunk sitting on the ramp in Burbank. But it's like Al said, "Bob, you can't remember everything!"

The next day we choppered over to the Atlantic side of the Canal Zone. We landed on a ball field at Fort Davis where we played for a rugged audience that had just crawled out of the jungle. The guys from the Second Battle Group of the 10th Infantry; the Latin-American School at Fort Gulick; and the Jungle Warfare Training Center at Fort Sherman. Standard issue for these guys is a pith helmet, two pairs of jungle boots, and a change of snakes.

What a reception they gave jokes like:

"This is where they train the men to survive in the jungle. It's really rough. You can't drink the water, the plants are poisonous, the insects eat you alive. However, some of the alligators are pretty good dancers.

"Everything grows in this lush, tropical climate. Last night I dropped an olive pit and this morning I had to fight my way around a six-foot martini.

"They just have two seasons here . . . rainy and dry. We missed the dry season. That was yesterday.

"It's so damp here, I can't tell whether you're applauding or splashing.

"But you guys are doing a great job guarding the canal. I understand you haven't let a ship through in years.

"They're having a few diplomatic problems here at the canal. Kennedy may ask Nixon to step in."

Delores Gay did a great flamenco number for the guys. She wore a sequined leotard and I must say she filled it well. The guys thought so, too. She used a rose as a prop and at the end of her number she teased the front row with it. And finally she gave it to one baby-faced Pfc and kissed him. I don't have to tell you the guys cheered—it sounded like the end of World War II.

I was watching backstage, waiting to introduce the next

number when I noticed that Janis Paige was watching, too! She seemed to be a little upset, so I asked her what was bugging her. Looking out on the stage where Delores was taking her third bow, Janis said, "How can I follow her?" Then she looked down at her own costume; a pair of levis, a T-shirt, and a straw hat. "They'll think I'm a boy. I can't go on, Bob, I just can't."

I've been in the business long enough to recognize a severe case of backstage nerves. There's only one way to handle it—you agree. "Okay, Jan," I said, "I'll go out there and make some excuse for you. The boys will be disappointed, but I know how you feel." I made a false start out toward the stage and nearly had my spine pulled out. She walked right over my back and out on the stage to the biggest ovation you ever heard in your life.

Janis is one of the most talented and dependable performers in the business. I like to think I discovered Janis. Actually, it isn't quite true. She was already on her way when we signed her to do a TV show in New York. We also had Arlene Dahl on the show. But that week Fernando Lamas came to town, and suddenly we didn't have Arlene Dahl on the show. With one quick rehearsal backstage, Janis took Arlene's part in a sketch, a dialogue piece with me, and did her own song and dance. Naturally, she was a smash or I wouldn't have even brought it up.

From there, she went into *Pajama Game* on Broadway and from there on it was all tax problems. How a girl with that much experience in front of an audience could possibly be nervous, I'll never know! Why doesn't she use pills, like I do?

It was a sweaty little group of PX pickers that hied themselves to the plane for the long flight out to Antigua.

Lieutenant Commander Austin Clark who was in charge of the aircraft and his co-pilot Commander Wen Brasser had a lot of time in the ready room. As a consequence, they were two very hot bridge players. Les Brown is also a big league bridge player (I knew there was something he could do). They needed a fourth for the game and, naturally, they picked me. I had the only seat with a table.

As we neared Antigua, the game got very intense. Thanks to Les's superior play and my wide-angled vision, we had the Navy on the hook for $1.35. By this time we were on final approach. The relief pilots flashed on the FASTEN SEAT BELTS—NO SMOKING sign, and it was too late for our senior pilot bridge players to go forward and take over. Maybe it's because there's a little chicken in all of us, but the next ten minutes were a study in hilarious frustration. With another driver in the seat, these two seasoned pilots were as nervous as two old maids on a roller coaster.

One turned stark white, and the other was billiard-table green. For a minute there it looked like containers for everybody.

You should have heard their dialogue.

"He's coming in a little hot, don't you think?"

"I didn't hear the wheels go down."

"I hope he knows he's only got four thousand feet of runway."

"He must think he's landing at Idlewild."

"Quarter flaps, you jerk! Quarter flaps!"

"I hope we walk away from this one."

What broke me up was that these were two million-mile pilots with hundreds of missions behind them. And the landing? It was perfect. I helped our two heros off the plane, dusted off their medals for bravery, and promised them I'd never tell a soul.

Antigua is a tight little British isle in the Lesser Antilles. In Nelson's day (the Admiral, not Rocky), it was an important naval base. Today it's primarily a missile tracking station with a small complement of military personnel.

We were met by a truck bearing a native steel drum band.

I'd heard these bands on albums, but I'd never actually seen one. It was quite a sight. The instruments are made from the tops of fifty-gallon oil drums. Then they heat and hammer these Texas tambourines until each section produces a different note.

You can imagine our amazement when they broke into a swinging chorus of "Thanks for the Memory." They'd never heard the release, so I hummed it for them. They ad-libbed it right back as though it was a full-band arrangement.

I enjoyed it immensely. Not only was the music great, but it made Les Brown nervous. Up to then he thought a fifty-gallon drum was something you drank out of.

I don't know whether the show was especially good that day, or whether the ninety people in our audience were starved for entertainment, but they wouldn't let us off. When we ran out of daylight, the guys there hustled up some flashlights and signal lanterns. We worked until there wasn't a live battery left on the island.

It's a good thing John Glenn wasn't in orbit that night. There wasn't enough juice left on the island to run a pinball machine.

Next, we headed for the most beautiful spot in the Caribbean Command—Ramey Air Force Base at Aguadilla on the eastern tip of Puerto Rico.

I'd always wanted to visit daiquiriville. They don't have any taxes there. In fact, I'd like to move there. But after I pay my taxes back home, I can't afford to.

Now that the Russian "tourists" are pouring into Havana, New Yorkers are all going to Puerto Rico. Now there's a switch!

It's no wonder the island is booming, it's really a vacationer's paradise. They have three kinds of weather there—golfing, swimming, and crap-shooting.

Every day is the same. The only way you can tell it's New Year's is when you wake up with a paper hat.

Les Brown, Janis Paige, and I ad-libbing by flashlight at Antigua.
(NBC photo)

Sugar is the principal crop, followed by pineapples, lemons, rum, tobacco, and embroidery work. You should try it. It makes a hell of a drink. These people really know what to do with a pineapple. They throw away the fruit and fill it with rum. It's the only way to fly. You can destroy yourself and get your vitamin C at the same time.

The air base itself is ridiculous. It's sort of a GI Beverly Hills. The quarters are brand-new, the grass is manicured, the landscape is lush with tropical plants. You can't tell where the golf course ends and the parade grounds begin.

I never will get over the Officers' Club. It makes San

Simeon look like a duck blind. It's the first time I've ever seen a bar with a control tower.

One wing of the dining room opens up and you can dance out over the Pacific. Which is pretty wild when you consider it's in the Atlantic.

All right, I'm exaggerating, but I knew one thing; I couldn't kid these guys about hardships. So in my monologue I talked about what a lavish place it was. I told them I was proud to be with the brave men who were helping to keep the world safe for legalized gambling.

I thanked them for the guard of honor that greeted me in full uniform—bikini, dark glasses, and a bathing cap at a rakish angle.

And I thanked General Greer for letting me watch the troops in review. I've never seen such surf-boarding.

I enjoyed doing the monologue that afternoon. There were thousands of guys with their wives and kids sitting on the grass around the stage. They were a wonderful audience. High on the hill, the coconut palms struck post-card poses.

While all was peaceful out front, Hurricane Zsa Zsa was building backstage. Actually, it all started the night before. Zsa Zsa was unhappy with the plush quarters assigned her, so she commandeered the twelve-room home reserved for the Commander-in-Chief, which at this time was President Eisenhower. But let's be fair about it: She needed all twelve rooms. Those diamonds take up a lot of space.

The morning of the show, Zsa Zsa had a few errands that needed to be taken care of. She needed a hair dryer from the beauty shop, which was closed. She wanted some additional towels from the quartermaster, who was lost in the audience waiting for the show to start. She needed some perfumed soap from the PX, which was closed. She needed a brighter light bulb, which the engineer would have to furnish. Before anyone knew what happened, our Hungarian Sergeant Bilko had all available vehicles in the motor pool tied up. It's a good thing nobody crashed on the run-way that day, the ambulance was full of Kleenex.

We may not be the most lavishly equipped troupe on the road, but on the other hand, we never considered ourselves hobo. We felt that with hairdresser Carol Meikle and our make-up man, Bill Morley, we were prepared for any emergency. It's customary for these two artisans to work back-stage where they can take care of all the girls in the show, and when necessary throw an eyelash or a dab of putty my way.

Zsa Zsa didn't see it this way. And being a woman of action, she promptly kidnaped Carol and Bill and locked them in her private fort.

Next she sent out for reinforcements. She drafted the Executive Officer of the base to hold the hair dryer over her head. I don't know whether he was an ex-flame thrower, or whether he was awed by her beauty, but he kept pointing the dryer in her ear. Finally exasperated, Zsa Zsa turned on him like a tiger and shouted, "Get out, Sonny! Maybe you could shoot a cannon, but with hair dryers you are nothing!"

Meanwhile, back in the dressing rooms, things were growing tense. Janis Paige, Anita Bryant, and Delores Gay are three very lovely girls with wonderful dispositions. When they found out Zsa Zsa had the hairdresser, believe me, the mascara really hit the fan.

I was working on stage and while the band was playing, Andy, singing, or Butch and Stumpy were dancing, I would sneak back and try to coax one of the girls out of the dressing rooms. Jimmy Hoffa couldn't have broken the strike. We had no choice, we sent two Air Police over to Zsa Zsa's and retrieved our hairdresser at gun point. Order was restored, and the show went on. Finally even Zsa Zsa deigned to grace our stage. She looked beautiful, but then I've never seen our Hungarian mantrap when she didn't look great.

And she really flipped the guys. We'd do a set routine and then, for an encore, she'd just ad-lib answers to questions from the audience. I don't recall all of her zingers, but here are a few that I made a note of:

QUESTION: What's more important, love or money?
GABOR: Love. Money doesn't help you in the evenings.
QUESTION: How do you feel about large families?
GABOR: I believe in it. Every woman should have at least three husbands.
QUESTION: Do you smoke or drink or anything?
GABOR: I don't smoke or drink.
QUESTION: Who are you going to marry next?
GABOR: You sound like my mother. I want a man who appreciates the finer things in life . . . diamonds, furs, and me.

I could go on like this for twelve pages, but you know how she hates publicity.

The following noon we were to play the naval station in San Juan. We had the night off so Zsa (if I may call her by her first Zsa), Janis, Jerry, Andy, Anita, and I hitchhiked a ride on an Air Force chopper and headed for the swinging capital of Puerto Rico.

Our gala evening didn't start out too gala. San Juan was jumping and we couldn't get a hotel room. Finally we tried the Caribe Hilton and Zsa Zsa got us all rooms. There's nothing like knowing who to marry. Judging from the business they were doing, Zsa Zsa doesn't have to worry about the alimony checks being late.

We helped her out with a few dollars on the gaming tables. Fortune didn't smile on us over the green felt, but it certainly did when we went out to hit a few of the night spots. Harry Belafonte was playing there and we caught his late show. I'd never seen "The Navel" work before and now I understand why he breaks attendance records wherever he goes. Andy and I got a particular kick out of it because we were doing a calypso parody on our show.

The next morning as our heads shrunk slowly back to size, we worked in the hot sun for the troops at Fort Buchanan.

Then, with headaches held high, we climbed back in our

plane and went island-hopping down the missle tracking range. We visited them all—Grand Turk, Eleuthera, San Salvador. They are leading an exciting life out there on the sand spits—every day a new cloud formation.

These guys are the Peeping Toms of the space age. They can see what's happening but they're not having much of the fun. Of course, it's not all electronic baby-sitting. Every so often a Walter Schirra, a Scott Carpenter, or a John Glenn will drop in unexpectedly. You have to expect that when you have a pool in your backyard.

In a day and a half we knocked off six shows. We played to sailors, Pan Am workers, dependents, and natives. We did shows for any size audience from eight to eight hundred. If the jellyfish could have applauded, we would have played for them, too!

It wasn't all work, we had our kicks, too. Especially in San Salvador where we were taken to four different markers where Columbus had positively landed. If they were all true, he must have waded ashore more times than General MacArthur! Finally, I turned to our native driver and said, "Are you sure that this is the spot where Columbus landed?" And with a beautiful innocent face he looked at me and said, "Absolutely, Mr. Hope. I remember it vividly. It was on Columbus Day."

The beach was loaded with beautiful conch shells and our whole crew turned pack rat. Janis Paige, who I think planned to wholesale them, waded out into the surf to wash off a prize shell. While she was bent over, a wave, which I had nothing to do with, caught her midships. She was washed up on the shore like a wounded grunion. Her hair was a mess and her two-hundred-dollar Dior gown was completely ruined. Stupid child! For a dollar and a half, I would have sold her one of my shells.

During the year prior to this trip, I had done quite a few jokes on Mr. Castro. Little daggers that might indicate to him that I'm not exactly a member of his fan club. Things like:

"I don't know why Castro is so sore at America. He wasn't that bad on the Jack Paar Show.

"He's doing a wonderful job down in Havana. He's making Tiajuana look like Vatican City.

"No wonder he's got that beard. He doesn't trust himself with a razor.

"I'm fascinated by the way he dresses. He looks like an Ivy League voodoo doll."

Somehow these jokes didn't seem too funny as we neared Cuba and the control tower warned our pilot to stay in the corridor or we'd be in danger of being fired upon.

Once both planes were safely on the ground, things seemed less nervous. Before Castro, Guantánamo Bay was one of the plushier assignments. It had all the accouterments of a fighting naval base: fine golf course, two heated swimming pools, lawn tennis courts, open air and hardtop theatres, shuffleboard and bocci.

Now all of that is changed. The buildings are still there but the attitude is different. The base is on a 24-hour combat alert.

Convoys of Russian ships are unloading stock piles of arms and sealed crates at Havana. Russian "technicians" are pouring into Cuba by the thousands. That's an awful lot of manpower just to put up a maypole.

Every school kid knows the strategic importance of Guantánamo Bay. It's only 90 miles from Florida and 800 miles from the Panama Canal. It's the main support of our Atlantic Fleet and dominates the leeward passage to the Caribbean.

It's not our government's most impressive tax loss, but it's guarded like the Brink's plant. Better, I hope.

I rode the fence in a Marine helicopter. There's twenty-four miles of chain-link fence guarded by a twenty-four-

Zsa Zsa at Guantánamo. She's got so much they named her twice.
(*NBC photo*)

hour patrol of choppers, jeeps, and armed sentries with dogs. The only way you can get in is to be drafted.

The other side of the fence isn't any friendlier. The Cubans are constantly patrolling. I'll tell you one thing: That fence isn't going anyplace.

The base at Gitmo is completely self-sufficient except for the water supply, which is on Castro's side of the fence. It's kind of harrowing to know that your enemy has you by the ice cubes. One turn of the valve and it's peanut-butter mouth for everybody.

Nobody's been allowed off the base for the past two years. When a guy gets an eight-hour pass, he just turns over. There's no place he can go. If he wants to desert, he has to hide in the washroom.

That's one time we really had a captive audience and we took advantage of it. We did two big shows. One the day before Christmas and one on Christmas night. And how the guys turned out! Sailors and Marines came off the battle-wagons, destroyers, and troop carriers. They came off the ships, they came down from the hills, and they came out of the trenches to welcome us.

The Navy's a stickler for protocol. In the afternoon show, Captain Paul Bjarnsen, the Exec Officer of the Marines, introduced the Base Commander, Rear Admiral Edward J. O'Donnell, who introduced me. In the next show, to even things up, the Executive Officer of the Navy, Commander Robert Ingraham, introduced the Marine Commandant, Colonel Merritt Adelman, who in turn introduced me. The guys were very patient. They waited through all the formalities for the jokes—and we were loaded:

"Guantánamo—that's a Navy term meaning 'Hear you knocking, but you can't come in.'

"They call this place 'Gitmo'—that's short for Guantánamo. And when you're here, you want to make it as short as possible.

"It's wonderful to be here at Cape Canaveral's ashtray.

"This is the only base in the world where the guards don't say 'Friend or Foe?' They just reach out and feel your chin.

"I asked the base psychiatrist if the tension was getting the men here. He looked at me and said, 'Not at all and stop walking on my half of the ceiling.'

"This week five guys put in for a transfer to Devil's Island. One of them was the chaplain."

The audience was great. These jokes were about them and the trouble they faced every day. They were also very enthusiastic about a sketch we did, called "Farewell to Arms." This was based on a recent order of the Defense Department announcing that wives of servicemen at overseas bases would be returned home.

Naturally the service personnel were upset. I realize the government was trying to cut down, but I think this time they were eliminating the wrong forms. A man deprived of his wife—that's like sending out a general without a swagger stick. Somebody should've had a long man-to-man talk with the Defense Department and explained that an airmail letter can't cover everything.

Our sketch had Janice and Anita as two Waves and Andy and me as two dependent husbands. The audience loved this switch and we played it all the way.

For the finish, Andy and I would hide in the closet while the Air Police tried to find us. The smoke from Andy's cigar was supposed to give us away. I asked Al Borden to pump a little smoke through a crack in the door so it could be seen on camera. Yup, Al did it again. The temperature was a hundred and five degrees and Al filled the closet and the stage and the surrounding area for a quarter of a mile full of smoke.

It took two tanks of oxygen and a pulmotor to bring me back. When I opened my eyes, Andy Williams looked down at me and said, "Are you smoking more and enjoying it less?"

Christmas Eve we stole a few hours for a cast party. Jerry Egan, who manages the Officers' Club, really turned it on for us. His crew set up a wonderful bar, the hors d'oeuvres were magnificent and dinner was delicious. But somehow it was a very quiet party. Perhaps it was the tension. Maybe the rugged schedule and the heat had drained us. Then again, maybe we felt far from home.

The party broke up early and we went to midnight Mass. It was an inspiring service, but I was somewhat astounded at the sermon. The priest walked up and down the aisle à la Billy Graham. As we left the church, I said to our director, Jack Shea, "I never saw a priest work so close to an audience." Jack said, "He had to get close to the audience. We stole his public address system for our show."

We finished our big show on Christmas Day with Anita singing "Silent Night." But all was not calm and all was not bright. As we took off for home, we left three thousand guys down below defending our corner of Cuba and making sure the landlord doesn't break democracy's lease. But the odds don't discourage them. They're not at all pessimistic. Like they say, "We've never lost a PX yet!"

CHAPTER TWELVE

I won't keep you in suspense. We had a very successful trip to Russia. We made it back.

Our flight from America to Denmark was magnificent. When we arrived in Copenhagen, we were informed by Aeroflot (the Russian airline) that our flight to Moscow was postponed due to a blizzard there. We thought nothing of this at the time. Later we found out that there had been no snow in Moscow for two weeks. What the real reason for this delay was, we never did find 'out, but it gave us a chance to dig the nightclub scene in Victor Borgeville.

Never was a city more attractive, the lights brighter, the girls prettier, the food better. The schnapps flowed like it was a Scandinavian bar mitzvah. The Iron Curtain was very close and this was our last night. And we made the most of it. They tell me.

I'd like to apologize here and now to the manager of the Grand Hotel for running up and down the halls at four in the morning, yelling . . . "Hans Christian Andersen is a fink!"

The following morning we got the official nod. We raced to Kastrap Airport where we boarded the TU 104, Russia's new commercial jet airliner. It was a huge, sleek silver job with sweptback wings. Just parked it looked like it was doing about four hundred miles per hour.

The interior was another story. The seats were luxurious in size but the fabric covering them was pieced. The brass luggage racks looked like they were swiped out of Lucius Beebe's railroad car.

I'm no Donald Douglas, but in a modern-day jet aircraft, I fail to see the need for tulip vases.

The plane seats seventy, but actually there were only fifteen other passengers on board, all dressed in black. It looked like a shipment of Erich von Stroheims.

Our passports were checked three times. Once at the gate . . . once at the bottom of the ramp . . . and once again at the top of the ramp. This was to prevent us from changing identity halfway up the stairs.

Russia may boast of a classless society, but the airplane design is entirely capitalistic. There is a large tourist cabin, and up forward is a more luxurious first-class cabin. The seats were very wide. In Russia everything's built around Khrushchev.

Ursula Halloran and Arthur Jacobs, my press representatives, and I, along with a couple from the American Embassy, were ushered into the first-class cabin. Although everyone appeared to have the same type tickets, the Russians all stayed in the other cabins. I don't know whether they were scared, secretive, or just snobs.

My cameraman, Ken Talbot, and two of my writers, Mort Lachman and Bill Larkin, were flying in via Prague and we would join forces in Moscow.

The Russian pilots may not be the best in the world, but they're the most definite. When they take-off, they really take-off, whether your stomach is ready or not. Our TU 104 left the ground like a seagull with sore feet.

You don't have to worry about a seatbelt on take-off. The thrust virtually glues you to your chair. According to the altimeter in our cabin, we climbed steadily to thirty thousand feet. Here we leveled off and headed for Moscow at a speed of 500 miles an hour. The flight was smooth and, with the exception of my knees, there was no vibration.

I guess this was a Red, Red Carpet flight, because next came a meal served by our flight hostess. Her uniform was strictly out of *Vogue*, black coat and babushka. She spoke no English but she had a winning smile. I was always a push-over for steel teeth.

The first course was vodka, my first taste of the real thing. I don't know why they bothered to keep it in a bottle. They could have drained it directly out of the jet fuel tanks.

You've heard Smirnoff's slogan—"It takes your breath away." Russian vodka takes the breath and both lungs. Now for the first time I understood why there was an oxygen tube at each seat. It had nothing to do with the altitude.

The drinks were followed by a delicious steak and fresh vegetables. I didn't know it at the time, but this was the last edible food I was to have for some time. They must use Danish beef on all their jet flights. You could circle the globe three times while you're trying to get through a regular Russian steak.

After that came a hot beverage which was either tea or coffee. I hope it was either tea or coffee. And then—brandy, which I refused. Remembering the vodka, I shook my head "no." The hostess blinked her tooth at me. I was left with the feeling that I had lost my first diplomatic battle.

Before I had time to say "*sverdloff*," which is Russian for Tums, we were over Moscow. There was nothing subtle about our landing. The pilot just pointed the nose at the ground and let her rip. My ears popped three times on the way down.

Then we touched down. We lumbered along the runway for what seemed an endless amount of time. From the window I could see quite a few gleaming new jet transports. There must have been thirty of them. I wondered how long they'd be used as passenger planes.

The pilot cut the engines. Suddenly, all was quiet. I'd made it to Moscow. I'd tried harder to get there than Napoleon. I just hoped I wouldn't have as much trouble getting out.

Before we left the plane, they took our passports. A psychological maneuver designed to make you tremble. There is nothing quite so naked as an American tourist without his passport. The little green book with the U.S. seal commands world-wide respect and attention. And when they take it away, you feel like an international wetback.

As I stepped out of the plane into the intense cold, I lifted my head high and gave out with a big smile for the cameras. There were none.

I pulled my coat around me and headed for the administration building. As I fought against the wind and swirling snow, I looked up and saw something that made my day, a true Russian paradox. The windows of the control tower were festooned with curtains.

The building itself was a cozy little mausoleum. It appeared to be about two hundred years old, which is pretty old as airport buildings go. I was amazed to learn that it was relatively new. Later I learned this was true of many buildings constructed during the Stalin era. It seems that the Socialist man felt the need of a Gothic womb.

As I stepped inside, I was greeted by Irv Levine, whom I had met before only by telephone. And with him was his lovely new bride, Nancy. Irv took my picture . . . we became immediate friends. Nancy laughed at my jokes . . . soon we were inseparable.

Other members of the welcome wagon included Ed Stevens and Bob Sandberg of *Look* magazine . . . Serge Fleigers of International News Service and Eric Lessing, the famous free-lance photographer from Magnum.

For a nation that's got the original patent on bureaucracy, they've got a lot to learn about red tape. Customs was a breeze. I expected to wait three hours while they strained my toothpaste, sent my hair dye out for chemical analysis, and checked my monologues for Khrushchev jokes. They didn't even open a suitcase. Made me kind of sore at first. I swallowed those keys for nothing.

While I was filling out my customs declaration, there was quite a stir in the waiting room. An MVD man, wearing magnificent black leather riding boots, strode toward me. And the squeak of those boots was deafening. It was the only stereo I heard in Russia.

Handing me my passport, he said in a booming voice, "I understand Detroit is all closed down." I was staggered by this remark because there was an auto strike at the time. However, it was necessary to keep face, so, thumbing through my mental file of clichés, I replied, "Nothing serious—they just ran short of air-conditioning units." This was the start of an argument that was later completed by Nixon and Khrushchev.

I bowed to the onlookers and returned to my customs declaration. It was a simple form. "How much money are you carrying into the country?" The fools! If they'd read the ad, they'd know. "I never carry more than fifty dollars in cash."

Also, I guaranteed in writing that I was not bringing in any hashish, deer horns, or wormseed. And so, leaving my deer horns and wormseed behind, I climbed into my chartered Zim and headed for Moscow proper.

Our car (a reasonably exact facsimile of a 1938 Buick) was part of the Intourist plan. Officially, we were a delegation, but we traveled at our own expense and so used the Intourist program.

For thirty dollars a day, per person, we received a book of coupons which entitled us to de-luxe accomodations, three meals a day, tea, a chauffeur-driven car for two hours a day and the services of an interpreter. It's an excellent arrangement, although at thirty dollars a day, it hasn't as yet caught on with the peasants.

There are only two kinds of hotels in Russia. The pre-revolutionary type like the National, and the new hotels which look exactly like the National. We were assigned to the Ukraine Hotel, which was an exception to the rule. We were amazed at how modern it was. The Ukraine was completed in 1957 and looked like a Japanese copy of the Waldorf-Astoria.

The first five floors are lobby, which may very well have been elegantly furnished. I'll never know. The entire time we were there, most of the furniture was covered by sheets. The people's upholstery is not to be abused. Not even by the people.

The Ukraine is not a regular Intourist hotel but is usually reserved for the top agriculturists and leaders of trade delegations in the U.S.S.R. And as we walked in, the lobby was swinging with hundreds of pajama-clad Uzbeks and Mongolians, intent on a bacchanalian weekend at the ball-bearing works.

We were greeted at the desk by a pleasant young lady named Nina. She spoke just enough English to confuse us both. But after a good deal of sign language and winsome smiles on both sides, our party managed to get rooms on the same floor.

When it comes to crowding, the Moscow elevators begin where the New York subways leave off. The elevators belong to the people and they all try to use the same one at the same time. In the thirty-odd trips I made up and down, I don't think my feet ever did touch the floor. It was my first intimate contact with the Russian people. And this much I learned: garlic outsells Arpège.

In trying to describe my suite, I find it difficult to be fair. To a visiting fireman from Pinsk, it might seem rather luxurious, but the average American would expect something more from a big new hotel in the capital city. He'd expect and get more from a motel on Highway 66.

I had three rooms: a living room, a bedroom, and a bath. Yes, the plumbing worked. The bathroom was complete, but here again, as we know it, the fixtures were ancient in design and style.

At this point I'd like to bring up an indelicate subject. If you plan to visit the Soviet Union, bring your own tissue. It is not too good anywhere in Europe, but believe me, the Russians are the hardiest race of all.

From my room I could see the Kremlin, and vice versa. We were both up all night peeking.

One thing we didn't have to complain about was the lack of heat. The Russians know how to cope with cold weather. (It was 28° below while we were there and this was in March.) The windows had double-panes and all doorways to the building carefully shielded the lobby from any direct draft.

My room was one of the more lavish; it had a piano, singularly out of tune. It also had a twenty-inch television set, which was largely responsible for a joke that was widely quoted.

After I finished unpacking, we played the popular Russian tourist game, "Search for the hidden microphone." The TV set with all its wires was a very suspect place and we searched it thoroughly without finding anything.

Back in the States a reporter asked if they had television in Russia, and without thinking, I replied, "Yes. But it watches you."

That brings us to a question that I've been asked many, many times. "Were we spied on?" "Were our rooms bugged?" "Were we tailed?"

Truthfully, I don't know. After all the stories you're told and have heard, you expect to be.

Whenever I'd enter my room, I'd pound on the wall and yell, "Testing! Testing! One! Two! Three! Am I coming in loud and clear?" And whenever we were discussing anything that might in any way be misinterpreted, one of us would look up at the ventilator and holler, "Only kidding, Kru!" Whenever I left my room, I'd sign off by facing the wall and shouting, "That concludes our broadcast for this afternoon. We now present an interlude of organ music. Be sure and catch the late, late show, same time, same room." We were actually half-joking when we did this, but it was a joke only because there was a possibility that the Big Bear was listening.

We were told that the entire thirteenth floor of the hotel was loaded with tape-recording and monitoring equipment. We had no way of knowing whether this was true or not. The doors to the stairways were all locked and the elevators had no button for the thirteenth floor, which is pretty suspicious. On the other hand, neither does the Beverly Hilton, which leads to an obvious conclusion: either the Russians are superstitious or Conrad Hilton has a mighty interesting record collection.

As for the question, "Were we tailed?" I think not. That would really have been ridiculous. None of our little group spoke Russian; in fact, a government-provided interpreter was with us at all times. When we went anywhere, it was in a chauffeur-driven car, and most of our meetings were with high Soviet officials. I don't think the Russians ever really worried about us as spies. There wasn't a Peter Lorre in our whole group. It took us three days just to find the proper dining room.

Food. Sorry I brought that up. It brings back that first morning in Moscow. I awoke bright and cheery and bounced out of bed in my usual style. Usual style—that means I lowered my head to the floor and crawled to the phone like a caterpillar. I pulled myself up on one elbow, lifted the receiver and pleaded into the phone for Room Service. The answer was the longest razzberry I've ever heard.

It took a few minutes before I realized it was the dial tone. Then I remembered that the hotel had no switchboard. I'd have to dial Room Service. No problem here. I've been in a few hotels, they all have a list of the various shops and services. And I was right. There was one on the desk.

The printing seemed a little fuzzy, so I reached for my glasses. The printing was now clear and boy, was it fuzzy. It was in Russian. Frantically, I started dialing numbers at random. If anybody answered, I'd yell, "Orange juice and coffee!" I was getting desperate. Then there was a knock on the door. It was the maid. I smiled at her, the smile I reserve for producers, and in my most seductive manner, I whispered softly, "Orange juice and coffee." She took a step backward, then retreated down the hall. I followed, step by step, enunciating clearly, "Or-ange juice and cof-fee."

In front of the elevators we were intercepted by a lantern-jawed floor matron. The maid cringed behind her. The matron shouted something to me in Russian and indicated that I should return to my room. I don't know what she said, but I felt like Jack the Ripper. I pantomimed squeezing an orange and drinking. By now we had been joined by another maid, a porter, and three delegates wearing fezzes. I thought they might be Shriners, but they weren't carrying bags full of water. The crowd was growing.

I repeated my plea, "Orange juice and coffee." Suddenly, the porter smiled. He nodded understandingly and shook my hand. I returned to my room feeling like I'd just swung a summit meeting. Twelve hours later, when I arrived back in my room after dinner, my breakfast was there—an apple and a glass of tea.

I think I found the Achilles heel of the Communist system. If they have to call Room Service for the bomb, we've all got a few years to live.

Monday was our first full day in Moscow and we had our first appointment with the Soviet top brass.

In the lobby we met our interpreter, Larissa Soborova, a charming girl about twenty-two years old. She wore boots, a sheared sheep coat and her pride and glory, a blue angora babushka. And when I say she wore it, I mean she wore it —seven days a week, indoors and outdoors.

We knew that all the interpreters were official representatives of the government and presumably high in favor. Naturally, we expected some hard-core zealot who would drown us in a sea of propaganda. Not Larissa. She was a shy, quiet girl who was proud of her country and her job.

Evidently she was one of the best. She'd been assigned

to Adlai Stevenson, John Gunther, Cary Grant, and Mike Todd. As a matter of fact, the blue babushka was Mike's gift to her. She spoke perfect English, which led to considerable trouble. She couldn't understand us at all.

It's too bad Shirley MacLaine didn't have Larissa to smooth things over for her. When Shirley was in Russia on a recent trip, she missed her train from Leningrad to Moscow. When she got back to her hotel to get her room back, it was rented. When she got back to the depot, her luggage was gone. Shirley was pretty upset and I don't blame her. I know that insecure feeling you get when you're separated from your eyebrow pencil.

I don't know whether it was government policy or Larissa's natural reticence, but she showed absolutely no curiosity about the United States. She did ask where we were from and when we told her California, she said, "I understand the weather is lovely there." Which proves that the Russians aren't the only ones who've been successful with brainwashing.

No wonder Russia did so well in the Winter Olympics. When you step outside the door of your hotel in Moscow, you're skiing whether you want to or not. If you don't put your hat on slowly, you'll crack your ears.

I've never seen so much snow. The whole country looks like it was painted by Grandma Moses. Of course, I'm not exactly new to the cold—I've been to Alaska, Greenland, Iceland, and several Academy Award presentations.

Word gets around pretty good in Moscow. Without any instructions, our Russian driver seemed to know that we were meeting with Igor Rachuk, deputy chief of the cinema section of the Ministry of Culture. He drove us directly to the Soviet Export Film Building, a commercial-sounding name, but quite different in appearance when you approach it. It looked like a set for Foreign Intrigue. The walls were thick concrete, the kind you can't hear screams through. There were stone-faced, uniformed guards at the entrance who stared at us with sullen eyes. We were guilty; it was just a question "of what."

A gaunt old man, stolen from Dickens, took our coats. Then we crossed an open courtyard. I had the feeling there were a thousand pairs of eyes watching us. This was one time when I wasn't happy about the rating.

The rugs were threadbare, the stairs creaky. Suspicious glares followed us down the hall. It was as though we were walking the last mile to the brainwash.

We walked through five offices and seven doors before we arrived in Comrade Rachuk's office. He was waiting there with five movie heavies from Central Casting. Instead of Madison Avenue Gray, they were wearing Gorki Black.

Mr. Rachuk's first words were, "You are seven and a half minutes late." At this point I figured maybe I should tip over the table and make a run for it. He continued, "In Russia promptness is a virtue. Anybody who is late must pay a fine." I looked first at Mort, then at Bill, trying to decide which one I should leave as hostage.

Then Rachuk smiled for the first time and said, "As penalty, the men must drink the wine to the bottom of the glass and the ladies must eat the sweets to the bottom of the bowl."

In the excitement, I reached for a piece of candy and got a laugh I didn't expect to start off the conference.

We held a very interesting discussion on two levels. Most of the time it appeared we joked back and forth. Underneath, we were both doing a little international horse trading.

It's rather difficult to describe the meeting. It was almost like the first round of a fight. Everybody had their verbal dukes up but nobody was throwing any punches. I wasn't sure which man really had the power and I didn't know in which direction to throw my big smile.

They asked me exactly what I wanted. I explained that we would like to have a theatre filled with people that

would understand English where I could deliver a monologue and be assured of a few laughs. Also, I threw in a
suggestion that left them staring: I asked them if it would
be possible to arrange a forum with their leading theatrical
personalities where we could ask each other questions about
our mutual professional problems.

This I thought would be of great interest to our home
audience, but we found out later it didn't interest Mr. Rachuk. I don't know whether we didn't get through to him
or whether the man under the desk said "no." Anyway, the
whole meeting had a lot of cat-and-canary feeling. The only
thing we agreed upon was to disperse for the day. They
went into a huddle and we went out on a tour.

CHAPTER THIRTEEN

Our first stop was Red Square, the heart of Moscow—if Moscow has one. At the south end of the square is St. Basil's Cathedral with its nine onion-shaped domes, Russia's answer to Disneyland.

St. Basil's was built in the sixteenth century by Ivan the Terrible. Our interpreter was a bit vague on how he got that name, but it's a cinch he had a very low Trendex.

Ivan hadn't taken the Dale Carnegie course and had rather a difficult time getting along with people. It was in Red Square that Ivan put his enemies in iron cages and set them on fire. Thus justifying the claim that the Russians invented the outdoor barbecue.

To the west near the Kremlin wall is one of the most modern-looking buildings in Moscow. When I was there it was known as Lenin's and Stalin's tomb. That gives you an idea of the housing problem—you even had to share a tomb.

The mausoleum was the biggest show in Russia. The day was bitter cold. A deep breath was like inhaling an icepick. And yet, there was a line of people eight deep and a half mile long waiting to get into the tomb. And we were told that it was this way every day. Even discounting shills, a million people a year used to come to gaze upon these two still men. It's a shame Stalin had to move recently—for reasons that had nothing to do with housing.

There was a cordon of police marking off a large area around the tomb. We wanted to go in close and get shots of the people lined up. Not speaking any Russian, we couldn't ask for permission, so we decided to just walk through the line of police with our camera and see what happened. Nothing did. They paid no attention to us. However, when a few curious Russian civilians tried to follow us through, the police stopped them. It was almost as though word had been sent down from above that we were not to be bothered.

We went on a quick tour of the Kremlin, an area that covers some sixty-four acres. If it had been a golf course, we might all be sleeping better these nights.

The Kremlin wall encloses churches, museums, government offices, and the Grand Palace, where the party meets. It's hard to describe, but it looks like Charles Addams' answer to the Pentagon.

I don't know what the grand strategy of the party was that year, but as I passed an open door in the Kremlin, I heard a voice say . . . "Do you think that crackpot down in Cuba could be bought with a sugar loan?"

As part of the propaganda, all of the treasures of the royal families are now on view for the public. I saw one crown with over thirty-eight hundred large diamonds in it. It would have made a wonderful beany for Zsa Zsa.

Jack Benny asked me to bring back a fur hat with a part in it. So I crossed Red Square to visit the GUM department store. It was built under the Czar in 1893. I think the chocolate bar I bought was part of the original stock. Incidentally, the price for one bar of candy was a dollar sixty.

The store is one of the largest in the world. It comprises some four city blocks. It made Macy's look like the general store in Upper Sandusky.

I tried to buy one of those fur hats like I'd seen the men wearing on the street. Then I found out those aren't hats. That's the way they cut their hair.

Don't let anyone tell you that the Russians aren't passionate. At the perfume counter they displayed such sexy-sounding scents as "Kremlin" and "Our Moscow." I don't know how they missed "Moonlight on the Collective Farm,"

My fan club greets me in Red Square. (Look *magazine photo*)

"Volga Boatmen," and "Essence of Tractor." This one not only smells good, but it's wonderful for lubricating a fan belt. Instead of "My Sin" it's "Where Do I Go to Confess."

And if you want to bring a romantic tear to your girl's eye, send her a box of candy. They have a picture of a hydroelectric plant on the cover.

Russia's a great place if you want to give up smoking. Cigarettes cost just under a dollar a pack. There's about an inch of tobacco and three inches of filter. By the time the smoke reaches your mouth, you've kicked the habit. Khrushchev must like them long. At diplomatic meetings he can flick his ashes on anyone in the room.

The day we were there, GUM was having a big fashion show. It was not unlike our own American fashion shows.

The clothes in the show were the height of fashion. However, you seldom saw a woman on the street wearing anything even approaching this. The women bricklayers and the gals shoveling snow in the streets lean more toward Ma Kettle than Loretta Young.

This was a Sunday, the one big shopping day in Moscow. The stores and streets were jammed with lookers and a few feelers. The high prices stopped the actual buyers.

Everywhere we went we were immediately recognized as foreigners. Alongside the drab black attire of the Russians we must have looked like Martians in our colorful clothing. Everywhere we went people stared. Of course, the same thing would happen if Bulganin showed up on Hollywood Boulevard wearing a fur hat. People would think he was an "extra" in a George Pal movie.

I was stopped only once by a bright-eyed eleven-year-old boy who said, "Hey, American, you got any postal cards of New York?" I whisked the urchin into a side alley and traded him a stick of gum for a little pin commemorating the 40th anniversary of the revolution. You wear it on your lapel and it guarantees you free admission to any Congressional investigation.

No Russians appeared to recognize me. I don't know whether it's because my pictures haven't played there . . . or because they have.

When the Russian tourist officials were told that I was coming, they asked, "Is that a male or a female?"

Every once in a while a Mongolian or a Chinese would walk past, then do a take, and then grin at me in a friendly way. I'm not sure why. Maybe they saw my films in China before the Communists took over, maybe my pictures paved the way.

At Sverdlovsk Square I visited the pride and joy of Moscow, one of the underground stations of the Metro or subway. These stations are magnificent. The marble walls are lined with beautiful murals, porcelain, and bas-reliefs. It's

The cutest doll I met in Russia—or Smoking more and enjoying it less.
(*United Press International photos*)

like a drive-in movie for trains. Actually, it's a wonderful idea, you can get an art education while you're having your ribs broken.

The Metro belongs to the people and they keep it spotless. A litterbug is liable to be nudged into the third rail. Two million passengers a day ride the subway and there isn't a wad of gum in sight. How backward can you get?

Emerging from the subway, I met a little old lady selling the Russian version of Eskimo pies. She was doing a swinging business despite the fact that it was still below zero. I

Eliot Ness reviewing the cast of The Untouchables. (*United Press International photos*)

asked her if she wasn't afraid her ice cream bars would melt. She turned to a companion and said something in Russian which I took to mean, "No wonder they're so far behind in the missile race."

As in cities all over the world, whenever we started to film, we collected a crowd. In Sovietskaya Square we set up our camera presumably to take pictures of the monument of the founder of Moscow. Before the tripod was up, we had an audience of over a thousand people. Half of them were just curious about our equipment and the other half were probably waiting to see us get arrested.

We had to be careful. As soon as you turned a lens on the people, they turned away. It was almost as though the whole country was on the lam. When you walked on the street, the people never really turned and looked at you. They sort of caught your act out of the corner of their eye.

Some of the faces were wonderful, especially the kids. We wanted to get them on film without making them self-conscious. I would pose near the statue and Ken Talbot would aim at me. When everybody was concentrating on me, Ken would pan down and take the faces. I hope you saw them on the show. They were beautiful.

The crowd and activity were commencing to bug a burly cop on the corner. I could see him making up his mind. Just as he started toward us, Ken turned the camera toward him and I pantomimed for him to continue directing traffic. Ham is universal. While he went into his act, we packed our gear and got the hell out of there.

The next day I met with the Minister of Culture himself, Nikolai Mikhailov. We opened our business meeting with a discussion of the American-Soviet hockey game which the Russians had won. The Minister got a great charge out of the victory and was in a jovial mood. He asked me if there was anything he could help me with.

I explained my needs for the television show and asked again for the use of a theatre. He parried this, referring it to Mr. Rachuk, who sat on his left.

Next, I asked to meet the Russian film stars. They suggested a cocktail party and a date was set for this. I asked for a chance to talk to their English-speaking students at the university. They agreed that it was a wonderful idea, but somehow the date for this was never set. I also asked if it would be possible to see the movie and television studios. Not only would it be possible but desirable and would be

233

arranged immediately. "Immediately" takes a little longer in Russia. I still haven't been there.

I asked for some film clips of the top Russian stars. I explained how interested Americans would be in seeing them, and that it might be a fine example of the Soviet-U. S. Cultural Exchange. Mikhailov said, "Certainly. There'll be a price, of course." My wallet blanched—that kind of talk always makes me nervous.

After the meeting we adjourned to what I imagined was a very comfortable projection room. Once again the furniture was shrouded with white sheets. Here we saw endless reels of color film: variety shows, youth pageants, and patriotic exhibitions. An example of this was a beautiful color film of a government-sponsored Christmas party for the children. This party was in Leningrad but it was designed to give everyone in Russia the feeling they were there. It's great if you dig a canned Christmas.

Perhaps to remove the religious connotation, Christmas no longer exists officially. The kids celebrate New Year's with New Year's trees. And Santa Claus looks like our Santa Claus but he's called Grandfather Frost.

During the viewing, we would indicate what portions of the film we thought we could use. We made notes, but Comrade Rachuk merely nodded absently. When it was over, I asked if he'd like a copy of our notes. He just laughed and proceeded to rattle off the thirty-five film clips complete with the exact footage. Yet the next day when we returned for a further conference, it was as though we were meeting for the first time. All discussions started as though none had been held. We were shown the same film that we had seen the day before. I didn't know whether this was deliberate strategy or accidental, or whether they're quicker than we are on reruns.

When I returned to my hotel room from the first meeting, I found that my suitcase was open and that my monologues were spread out on the bed. These were all jokes about

Russia. Some I had done on radio; some on television; and some I would never do anywhere. There were over five hundred different kinds of jokes, but these will give you a general idea:

"They have a national lottery here. It's called living.

"But the workers love Khrushchev very much. He hasn't got an enemy in the entire country. Quite a few under it.

"Mikoyan is number two man in Russia. Number two . . . that means if anything happens, he gets to sit with the driver when the bus leaves for Siberia.

"No wonder they've invited Van Cliburn to Moscow. Khrushchev thinks he has the secret plans to a hair mine.

"Following his doctor's orders, Nikita has cut his drinking in half. He's leaving out the water.

"And everywhere you go here in Moscow you see soldiers. It looks like recess at Little Rock High School."

I still don't know who went through those jokes and I guess I never will unless Molotov starts doing my act in Pinsk.

It gave me an eerie feeling knowing that my material might have been microfilmed, and now playing at my neighborhood MVD station. I didn't know whether to put the jokes back in my suitcase or run down the hall and plant them in somebody else's room.

A few minutes later I was soaking in a warm tub when a rather forlorn and bedraggled Chester Conklin stumbled into my room. While I attempted to hide my massive figure behind a bar of soap, he calmly introduced himself as a reporter from the Moscow *News*.

I hurriedly climbed into a robe and made myself available for his questions. For a reporter he was a bit unusual in that he had no questions. He checked the Soviet tourist guides that we had bought in London and threw them on the floor, claiming they were junk.

Then, while I launched into an eloquent and witty soliloquy on my impressions of Moscow, Chester checked the closets and tried on all my clothes. He interrupted just once to ask if I would mail him some paperback mystery stories with pictures of girls with big bosoms on the cover.

Then, clutching my favorite cravat to his chest, he promised to return and fled into the dusk of the hall. Somewhere in Russia tonight there's a happy peasant spilling borscht on one of my Countess Mara ties. And he wrote nothing about me in the paper. So much for payola in Russia.

The phone rang and Jack Rourke, a West Coast TV personality, came in loud and clear from Los Angeles. I guess they have to have plenty of power on those Russian phones . . . there's a lot of people listening.

I don't know how Jack managed to locate me, for there are no phone books issued in Moscow. It's like Beverly Hills . . . only the whole country is unlisted.

Jack has a radio show called "Party Line" and he arranged a world-wide conference call with the cast of *Paris Holiday*. He had Martha Hyer on from Los Angeles, Anita Ekberg from New York, and Fernandel from Paris.

There was a lot of static on the line and communication was virtually impossible. Somehow Ferny's pantomime just didn't get through.

The best part of the call was the finish. The long-distance operator asked Jack to whom the call should be charged. And Jack answered, "Send the bill to the Kremlin." The operator must have taken him seriously because Jack was never billed for the call. I don't know if the Kremlin was upset about this, but on the tenth of the month Beria was executed.

Not having the technical crew we'd anticipated, everybody in our little posse had to double. We'd brought our own film and Arriflex cameras from England. Every evening we'd gather in the hotel room and take turns reloading the film magazines. It's not that I don't trust Mort and Bill, but it seems like my turn came around awfully fast.

The severe cold made the film very brittle and we lost

more than a few of our best shots that way. The exposed film was carefully replaced in tins, marked, and sealed with tape.

We'd heard many rumors that the Russians might tamper with film which they hadn't processed. It would be easy to do. If someone lifted the lid and exposed the footage to daylight, we'd be out of show business. We guarded the film and kept it under lock and key. But until we returned to the lab in Los Angeles, we'd have no way of knowing.

At first we ate in the grand dining room just off the main lobby. This was a huge plaster cavern—an extremely cold room. And so was our reception.

After two days it was explained to us that this room was for von vivants, cash customers, and that there was a special dining room for those who used Intourist coupons. This room was a slightly smaller tomb in the basement of the building.

The maître d' wasn't overjoyed to see us, but we took this to be the universal maître d' attitude. After three meals here, it was explained to us that we were still in the wrong dining room. Although we were booked through Intourist, we were officially a delegation and would have to eat in the dining room so reserved. In what turned out to be our official dining room there were indeed many delegations from all parts of the republic. Each delegation had its own table with a small flag representing its country.

Our table had no flag. And just to see what kind of a fuss we could stir up, we demanded an American flag on our table.

This was more difficult than it sounds because we had no means of verbal communication. We usually invited our interpreter to dine with us. I don't know whether it was government policy or my manners, but they always declined. We had to get our message across with grunts, wild motions, sign language and a good deal of saluting. It looked like a bad night on "Pantomime Quiz."

But the next morning our flag was on the table. I know it sounds silly, but we were all kind of proud of it. When the other delegates all nodded and smiled, we felt we had won our first diplomatic victory.

Tuesday night the Levines and the Stevens invited us out to dinner at the elite Praga Restaurant. I didn't want to impose, but you know how it is when the rest of the gang wants to save a buck.

Praga was a crowded series of narrow rooms about a half level below the street. It was no Romanoff's, but then it wasn't exactly a Duffy's Tavern either.

A gypsy group was blowing up a storm and the tables were crowded. The lighting wasn't exactly romantic—fluorescent on white tile. But nobody seemed to mind. There were lots of women, but none you would turn to look at. And they don't call me swivelneck for nothing.

Most of the men wore suits but occasionally you'd see a husky chap in overalls. This was a carry-over from the days when the worker was idolized in propaganda.

Ursula Halloran caused a sensation on that night. She wore a low-cut gown and shoes with rhinestone heels. Everybody in the restaurant found an excuse to go past our table. They stared at those rhinestone heels as though they were something left over from the Czar.

There are no nightclubs per se in Moscow. Restaurants with dancing are the closest thing to it. The average bigwage earner or bureaucrat can't buy a car or a television set, so his only outlet is a swinging evening on the town.

Actually, it doesn't matter where you eat in Moscow because every restaurant has the same official menu. This is an eight-page affair in a heavy glassine cover. There are some hundred and one dishes listed in four languages: Russian, German, French, and English. Ordering is thus very simple. You make your selection from a hundred and one items and point at it in English. The waiter looks at it and repeats it in Russian. He nods with a smile, indicating you made a brilliant choice and disappears into the kitchen. A half hour later he reappears, shrugs his shoulders and asks what else you'd like.

Our host suggested that inasmuch as we had "American stomachs," we'd better play it safe and order chicken Kiev. According to the menu, this is a succulent hen stuffed with melted butter. It turned out to be almost that. From then on we learned that chicken was the thing to order if you wanted to make peace with your stomach.

I ate so much fowl that in case of an emergency I could have flapped my way back to Copenhagen.

The government is pushing wine, but judging from the other tables, and under the other tables, vodka is still the number-one drink. It's like Coca-Cola is in America. Only *you* curve instead of the bottle.

The Russians understand drinking better than we do. Along the highways they have sobering-up stations. If a comrade has downed too much juice, he is taken for a bath, coffee, and a little snooze. It's sort of an AA AAAA. Instead of a neon sign they have an ice bag hanging in the window.

Serge Fleigers of INS told us there was an all-girl orchestra playing at the Leningradskaya Hotel. This we had to have on film.

Although the Kremlin understood that we were going to take pictures in and about Moscow, it didn't exactly cover marching into the main ballroom of the leading hotel and shooting the floor show. Under these circumstances, there was only one honorable course to follow: we smuggled the camera in under Ken's coat.

Serge laid a few kopecks on the waiter and we got a table fairly close to the bandstand. By the time our wine arrived, the girls had klumped back on the stand. Our Russian Ina Rays were quite a bevy, two tons of the sweetest music this side of the Volga.

The girls ripped into a swinging arrangement of the ever-popular "When My Tractor Smiles At Me" and in no time the dance floor was a wild melee of boots and galoshes. I nudged Ken, he pulled out the camera and started a slow walking pan up the main aisle. I tried to shield him and walked right into the maître d'. He looked like Rasputin's keeper. Pointing a finger at the camera, he yelled, "*Nyet! Nyet! Nyet!*" Having caught Gromyko's act, I knew what this meant. He advanced toward us.

Drawing myself up to my full height, I retreated at once to the table. As he stood glowering over us, Ken put the camera on the chair and covered it with a napkin, indicating the episode was over. Playing it nonchalant, I filled a glass with wine, raised it in toast and said, "*Nazdarovia!*" which, freely translated, means, "How do you get out of this chicken country?"

Dracula then took up a position, folded his arms and dared us to make a false move. We held a fast summit meeting. Ken needed about five minutes to get a group shot of the band and four or five close-ups.

Serge spoke fluent Russian, so we used him to bait the bull. He stormed over to King Kong and shouted, "These people are guests of the Soviet Government! They have been brought here to take these pictures! Take me to your leader!" The huge hulk of a man visibly quaked. In a land where there's only one employer, it doesn't pay to take a chance. He meekly turned and led Serge out of the dining room and into the hotel manager's office.

We flew into action. Mort grabbed the lenses, Bill grabbed the tripod, I lugged the battery. Within three minutes Ken had all the shots we needed.

A few moments later Serge was back. He fought to a draw in the hotel manager's office. The matter would be taken up through channels and inside of a month or so, we should have a definite yes or no. We smiled like good losers, under-tipped in our usual chic manner and left quietly.

I hope you caught the gals on our show. That one minute of film was quite a hassle.

Right here I'd like to say a few words about Serge and our other newspapermen behind the curtain. Theirs is undoubtedly the most difficult assignment in the fourth estate. In addition to the constant harassment of their reporting assignment, these guys do a hell of a job of selling America. All of America's missile failures were reported in huge headlines by the Russian press. But when America launched its first Sputnik, there wasn't a single mention of it. Serge and the guys jumped on the phones and called the Propaganda Bureau, the news agency Tass, *Izvestia,* and *Pravda.* They challenged the editors, demanding to know whether they were propaganda organs or real newspapers. The next day our Sputnik was announced on page two.

Serge has since been transferred to Paris, so I guess it's all right to tell this story. He was a bachelor and quite lonely. Since television isn't the complete answer for a normal, healthy male, his thoughts wandered to girls. Not speaking Russian, it was very difficult to meet any. It's amazing how fast and how fluently this young man learned to speak Russian. He met a lovely young woman and they became very good friends. They went together for three months. One Saturday evening they had a date and when Serge went to pick her up, she had vanished without a trace. Her apartment was bare, there was no forwarding address. When Serge checked with the landlord, he was told that there was no record of any such person ever having lived there. Serge is in Paris now and I'll bet he's parlaying French like crazy.

Speaking of girls, I have to tell you this story about Arthur Jacobs. Like most press representatives, Arthur is a very enthusiastic man. He was one of the prime movers in getting us all excited about going to Moscow. When we got there, I found out why. He had the phone number of a Russian girl who lived just outside of Moscow. Here's a guy with a thousand numbers of glamorous girls in New York and Beverly Hills, but what proved to me that girls were here to stay was the fact that Arthur would travel all the way to Russia in fifteen-below weather to dial a number to see who picked up the receiver on the other end.

Arthur was the press representative on our picture *Paris Holiday* and saw the best in Paris. Although I didn't see her, Mort tells me that the girl he dialed in Moscow and met later at a vodka pub looked a little like a linebacker for the Green Bay Packers. Arthur said "Hello," bought her a drink, pushed her into a droshky, said "Good-bye," rushed to the hotel, packed and was down in the lobby checking out when I intercepted him and said, "Where are you going, Arthur, Stalingrad?"

He said, "I'm going back to London."

"Did you call the girl?"

He said, "Yes, I did and she beat me two out of three falls. I gotta get outta here. The food is lousy, the portions are too small, and the girls are too big!"

And thus our six-men crew was five.

CHAPTER FOURTEEN

The second night in Moscow, our Ambassador, Tommy Thompson, tendered a very handsome cocktail party in our honor. A bubbly affair marred only by one small incident. When I was introduced to Mrs. Thompson, the Ambassador's wife, she shook my hand enthusiastically and said, "Oh, I'm so glad you're here. I've laughed so many times at your wonderful show. Did you bring your violin?" I laughed gaily, and wandered down the reception line hoping that one of the Russians might be friendlier. I don't know whether she meant it or was just putting me on, but the hospitality certainly paid for the bruise.

When Ambassador Tommy Thompson discovered we were having trouble getting a theatre where we could do our show, he came to the rescue and offered us the Spasso House, which was the Ambassador's official residence.

It was a perfect spot and would seat all the English-speaking tourists in Moscow. We decided to use a large hall which during the Czar's era was a very festive ballroom. The afternoon we went to look at it, the kids from the American colony were taking ballet lessons there.

The Embassy staff really pitched in for us. They built camera platforms, threw up a fast stage and rounded up every stray chair in the diplomatic community. Thursday afternoon, it was standing room only all over town.

We had asked for our Russian camera crew to arrive at noon. They showed up at four. Their equipment was, to say the least, outdated. But the crew itself was amazingly expert and extremely efficient.

Within an hour after they arrived they had their cameras set up and were ready to go. At home we would allow three to four hours for setup. They not only had their four cameras set up, but they had the lights in place and the microphones installed and balanced. We were ready to roll.

We had an interpreter available at every camera position, but as it turned out, this was unnecessary. The language of film seems to be universal. Mort indicated the shot he wanted by pantomime and they understood immediately. He used only two words "Kamera" to start the cameras rolling and "Halt" to stop them.

One incident puzzled us at the time. We had brought forty thousand feet of film from England especially for this purpose. We wanted to use our own film so that it would be processed in our labs at home. Comrade Bessmertni, their head cameraman, said that our film jammed in their cameras. At the last minute they called their studio and had their own film sent over. This meant they would have to process the film and it would be out of our hands while in their lab. We were justifiably nervous. It's like waking up and finding your wife going through your pockets.

Due to the limitation of chairs, only about two hundred guests were invited. Most of them were from the Canadian, British, and American Embassies. However, by show time over three hundred had arrived.

The diplomats have a code of etiquette all their own. If an uninvited guest arrives at the front door, they can be ejected bodily without fear of an international incident. However, once inside the house, protocol demands that the intruder be cordially welcomed as a guest. And we played host to a gay little group of gypsies. Our audience was speckled with turbans, top hats, fezzes, burnooses, serapes, mantillas, saris, and loincloths. It looked like a Hong Kong bus station.

Sometimes a monologue goes well, other times it bombs. Maybe it's the performer, maybe it's the material, maybe it's the audience. This time they all seemed to jell. And we got some very happy footage.

The first few minutes on the stage are the most nervous for a comic. By then you know whether you're going to have a show or a lynching. I always try to open with something directly related to the audience I'm working to. This time it was:

"It's exciting to be here with you democrats. You must be democrats or you wouldn't be here in Moscow."

Next I did a wild little joke:

"It's a thrill to be here in Russia. I know I'm in Russia, this morning my stomach got up two hours before I did and had a bowl of borscht."

I don't understand that one myself, but it made me laugh. And it's made audiences laugh all over the world. In London it was: "My stomach got up two hours before I did and had a cup of tea." In Tokyo, "My stomach got up two hours before I did and had a cup of Wonton soup." If you ever get out on the road, remember this one. It's still a virgin in Copenhagen, Vienna, and Dienbienphu.

After this came jokes about the cold, the sights in Moscow, the jet flight over, and this one about the language:

"Surprisingly enough, I'm not having any trouble with the language. Nobody talks to me."

This line received a very healthy reaction, because it was something the audience had lived with. Life in a foreign post at best is lonely. In Moscow there is almost no social communication with the people. I talked with diplomatic attachés who have been in Moscow for years and have never been invited to a Russian home. Part of it is the language barrier, part of it is the lack of housing, and part of it is the fact that many of the Russian people seem afraid to talk to foreigners.

I talked about Eric Johnston selling American movies to Russia:

"The Russians may find some of our historical movies

hard to take. If they see *War and Peace*, it's going to come as quite a shock that Napoleon was really chased out of Moscow by Audrey Hepburn."

And I talked a little about Russian television:

"Russian television viewers are a lot like Americans. They're crazy about Westerns. There's only one difference. They root for the Indians."

The most interesting reaction of all came from our Russian interpreters who were flabbergasted by our satellite jokes. Although the Russian papers headline their Sputnik, there are Sputnik stamps, toys, and magazine covers, the people seem hesitant to discuss it. If you mention it in a private conversation, there is a cold moment and the subject is quickly changed. When I mentioned even the word Sputnik or satellite in the monologue, the interpreters looked at me as though they expected lightning to strike. They could not believe that anybody would have the temerity to discuss a subject of this governmental magnitude. They'll talk about the price of food, the weather, even the housing shortage, but as soon as you mention anything at the policy level, everyone shifts into automatic brainwash.

After the show, Mrs. Thompson laid on the finest meal during our entire stay. The *pièce de résistance* were fresh cucumbers flown in from Finland. This may not seem like a wild treat to you, but this touch of green was greeted by the staff with the wild enthusiasm that a money salad would receive at Jack Benny's house.

The Ambassador and his lovely wife are really the host and hostess with the "mostest on the ball." I had the pleasure of meeting them both again at the luncheon for Premier Khrushchev at 20th Century-Fox Studios. We were all very impressed with the Thompsons. I can't imagine a more difficult diplomatic post and I can't imagine a man more qualified to handle it.

I tried to see as much of Russian show business as my limited stay would allow. And of course my first visit was to the circus. The Big Top is big business in Russia. They have government schools to train acts and a farm system that would be the envy of any major league ball club. The new acts work their way from the small circuses to the big time.

Moscow has at least one circus that runs all year. The night I was there, it was jammed. As usual, Uri Durov's bears stole the show. His family has been training them for over one hundred years. Uri has both the audience and the bears eating out of his hand. The high point of the act is when he puts his head inside the bear's huge jaws. I wouldn't even try that with my agent.

Two clowns got one of the big laughs of the show. When a dog ran across the circus ring, the first clown said, "There's a Sputnik dog." "No, our Sputnik dog is up there," said the second clown, pointing toward the sky. "But this is an American Sputnik dog," the first clown replied.

This was the first and only Sputnik mention I heard, and, strangely enough, the only mention of America I heard on the stage.

The most famous and certainly the most delightful of clowns is Oleg Popov. I first saw and met him when the Russian circus was playing in Brussels.

Popov is the idol of Russia in much the same way Will Rogers was in this country. Kids imitate his baggy pants, floppy checked hat and blond Dutch-boy hairdo. We even saw a comic Popov hockey team, which wears the Popov costume and tours like our Harlem Globetrotters.

If I live to be forty, I don't think I'll ever forget my visit to the world-famous Bolshoi Theatre. It's the showplace of Moscow and its magnificent ballet and opera are very potent weapons in the prestige propaganda war.

The theatre is government-owned but self-supporting. This isn't too much of a problem, the SRO sign is always out, and at eight bucks a copy.

A tourist can always get a seat, but if you're one of the

locals, you go way to the end of a long, long line. Go figure a crazy, mixed-up country where ballet outsells boxing. I wouldn't be surprised if their wrestling was on the level.

The night I ducked in was for the premiere of the new ballet called *Spartacus*. This was a wild extravaganza with hundreds of beautifully costumed extras, cannons roaring, and on-stage explosions. I don't know whether this was their regular type of thing or whether they were trying to cover up a rocket launching.

The show was a little short on plot and a little long on mechanics for the critics. The next day they John Crosby-ed all over them.

Ballet and opera are "safe" topics and everybody in Moscow, in his way, is a critic. The performance was freely discussed all over town, pro and con.

However, the theatre's premiere ballerina, Galina Ulanova, is the universal favorite. This fifty-year-old People Artist is a symphony of grace and beauty, one of the most stunning performers I have ever seen on a stage. We were privileged to be able to bring her to the American television audience. Too bad she doesn't work with balloons, I might be able to book her in Vegas.

At a variety show I saw two brothers doing a satire on our gangster movies. This was hilarious and done with all the taste and wit of Sid Caesar. On the same bill was a puppet act in which toy dogs compared Moscow restaurants by what they found in the garbage cans.

The Russians flip over puppet shows. The most famous being Sergei Obraztsov's State Puppet Theatre that is jammed every night in the year. What a racket! Money pouring in and no actors slicing up the bread. I tried hard to get those puppets for my show, but I'm afraid Ed Sullivan outsmiled me.

They had to drag me there, I've had about all the Howdy-Doody I can handle. When I got there, I had to pay three-fifty for a backless, fold-down aisle seat. But I never had occasion to lean back. Sergei presented his puppets in an "Unusual Concert." The audience laughed like it was on a string. The main character in the show was a temperamental star who kept an entire opera company waiting while he sprayed his throat. He even got down on his hands and knees to look for the proverbial lost collar button. The puppets were unique in that they were three or four feet high and were worked mechanically on a pole from below. They were capable of walking, talking, dancing, waving their arms, bowing at the whim of the operator. I hope my sponsor never finds out how this is done.

In music, more than in anything else, you could feel the Western influence. The Russians, just like the French, English, Italians, Japanese, and Poles, are crazy about American jazz.

Russia boasts full employment and at least half of those employed must be musicians. In every hotel and dining room there's usually one or two bands. And they were all making rather pathetic attempts to swing, but like it wasn't making it, man.

The Soviet Government has made its position very clear. American jazz is decadent. Yet the first time I walked into a hotel dining room, the band was blowing "Lullaby of Birdland."

American jazz records are one of the hottest items on the black market. A Louis Armstrong, Benny Goodman, or a Glenn Miller album will bring as high as a hundred dollars. Next time I visit Moscow I'm gonna have me some round flat luggage.

One pink evening, after downing my share of potato juice, I hired the hotel band and led them to the house of *Look* correspondent Ed Stevens. This trio, piano, guitar, and bass, was one of the best jazz combos I'd heard over there.

The piano player begged me to send him some of the latest jazz arrangements. As soon as I got back, I had Les Brown send as many as possible. I don't know whether they were received or not. If you're ever in Moscow, keep your ears tuned for three gypsies wailin', "I've Got My Love to Keep Me Warm."

Although the musicians spoke very little English, they were anxious to learn the latest jazz lingo. Even George, Irv Levine's interpreter, was fascinated by hip jazz talk. I exposed him to our crewcut Bill Larkin, and George will never be the same. One night after a tumbler of vodka, George stood up and shouted, "Let's split, man, this scene is wigging me."

As an interpreter, George gets two hundred and twenty-five dollars a month. They're going to have to pay somebody five hundred dollars a month to understand him.

Television in Russia is still in its infancy. They haven't even fired a comedian yet. I tried the set in my room several times but couldn't get a picture. I found out later the set was all right, but the stations are only on a few hours a day. They have two channels in Moscow and no commercials. Stop packing! Instead, they have lectures on crop rotation, basket weaving, and confessions. If you're lucky, you might catch a hot chess game on the coax from Omsk.

A twelve-inch set costs around seven hundred dollars, so most viewing is a group affair. I walked down the hall at the National Hotel and passed a group of chambermaids and waiters all crowded around the TV set in the lounge. They were watching an old movie. I suddenly had the feeling I never left home. I was gripped by a deep nostalgia for Channel 13.

Movies are still big business in Russia. But so far they have seen very few American films. The few that have been admitted are stories like *On the Waterfront*, *Wetback*, and *Blackboard Jungle*. All films calculated to depict strife, discrimination, and poverty in America.

They have never been allowed to see such classic examples of fine entertainment as *Bachelor in Paradise*, *Road to*

Hong Kong, and *Critic's Choice.* I pity these poor, under-privileged people.

My last day there I was invited to a cocktail party at the Ministry of Culture. Here I met three of the Soviets' most glamorous film stars. First was Skobtsova, a very fine dramatic actress. She achieved fame for her role of Desdemona in Othello. Next was a five-foot blonde called Shivalova. She is a comedienne of the Imogene Coca variety. The third one was a Junoesque actress with a wonderful marquee name, Cherednichenko. She's a glamour star from the Ukraine, their equivalent of Anita Ekberg, only more so.

I don't know whether they had ever heard of me or not, but they greeted me warmly and gave me the visiting fireman smile. They were certainly not amateurs when it came to publicity pictures. They took my arms coyly and upstaged me right out of *Pravda.*

These gals could hardly be called glamorous in our sense of the word. They were a little closer to Sears than Ciro's.

High necklines were the uniform of the day. The furniture isn't the only thing in Russia that's slip-covered. I hate these old-fashioned actresses who make it with talent.

The girls spoke very little English and since I spoke no Russian, the only one who ended up with a date was our interpreter.

However, the girls did understand "Hollywood" and I achieved a certain luster just from having been from there.

Next came the darkest moment of our entire trip. It was time to talk money. I was led to a small office where a discussion was begun with Mr. Rachuk, Deputy Chief of the Cinema Section.

Following this impasse, I was led to the office of Michael Fadeyev, Deputy of Film Export. Following this impasse, I was led to the last office they had, that of Aleksander Davydov, head of Soviet Export Film.

With a good deal of paraphrasing, anguish and word

251

groping, and parrying, the same conversation took place in each office.

Two things were on the agenda; censorship and loot. I didn't have my tape recorder, so I'll have to wing this from memory. After the amenities and the opening bell, Davydov opened with, "Mr. Hope, the monologue which we have in our lab is magnificent, a thing of beauty, a rare treasure. But there are just a few jokes which might better be left out."

I explained to Comrade Davydov that we had not come to Moscow to defame Russia or proclaim it. Our business was comedy. All we wanted was to do a good show. I asked him for his specific objections.

Referring to notes in front of him, he listed the following jokes:

"I got a wonderful welcome at the airport. They fired twenty-one shots in the air in my honor. It would have been nicer if they'd waited for the plane to land.

"The Russians are overjoyed with their Sputnik. It's kind of weird being in a country where every ninety-two minutes there's a national holiday.

"Anybody without a stiff neck is a traitor.

"It's the big topic of conversation every place but the dog show."

The word traitor especially bothered Mr. Davydov. He said, "Traitor is a very serious charge in Russia." I knew what he meant. I suggested that this was a joke, not an accusation. I've had this problem with other audiences. "We are not implying that Russians are traitors," I said. "What we are trying to do is to state in a humorous way how proud the people are of their Sputnik. Exaggeration is one of the basic forms of comedy."

He considered this for a moment but was not convinced. "Perhaps you could eliminate all reference to the Sputnik. It is not really a subject for comedy."

Again I reiterated, "We are anxious to cooperate, but we

must be reasonable. Satellites and missiles are a big topic in Russia just as they are in America. We both lose if we treat you differently than any other country in the world." Then I told him some of these jokes that we had done on our last show in America:

"I guess you heard the big news from Cape Canaveral. Our government has launched another submarine.

"Actually our test firings of missiles is going well. They hit the target every time. As a matter of fact, there's hardly anything left of Bermuda.

"Our scientists think they have located the trouble. The rubber bands keep breaking.

"Actually, we have nothing to fear. With a ten-second warning, our Army can launch a missile that would completely wipe out our Air Force.

"I can't understand what's holding up our missile program. It's the first time the government ever had trouble making the taxpayer's money go up in smoke."

Never did these jokes play any better. This was really their room. If they recorded this routine, by now it must be a best-selling album.

The atmosphere cleared for the moment and an agreement was reached in this area. I asked that they provide me with a written list of jokes that they would like withdrawn. I, in turn, would give their wishes serious consideration. Subsequently there must have been an official change of heart. The list was never delivered to me at the hotel.

Later, when I called to check on it, the gentleman who was to provide the list was out of the office. He was, as the saying goes, sick.

Next Mr. Davydov brought up the question of money. I asked for a drink. He seemed to think I owed them a fee for film clips, laboratory processing, and a film crew.

"Mr. Davydov," I pleaded, "this is an educational film. Why, the whole thing is a promotion for your great Russian artists abroad. It's practically a one-hour commercial. Don't you think this would come under the Cultural Exchange Program?"

Mr. Davydov reached for his drink. "Mr. Hope," he replied, "friendship is friendship, but money is separate. It is my understanding that you are strong and robust financially."

"After taxes," I explained, "we are all peasants."

"Tovarich," he said, shaking my hand. When I looked down, there was a bill in it.

It's a shame Mr. Davydov is tied up with the party. He'd make a hell of a capitalist.

We thrashed verbally for several rounds and when he finally took his knee out of my chest, I owed Russia twelve hundred dollars. That was three years ago, and I still do. Two of the film clips I ordered never showed up. When they do, I'll be happy to pay. Not cash, I'll put it on the Diners' Club.

The next day I packed to leave. I have never been more anxious to get home and yet I felt that there was so much that I hadn't seen.

Like everybody these days, I was extremely curious about this nation that dominates one third of the world's surface. At Christmastime when we were in Korea looking across the 38th Parallel into the Reds' rifle barrels, little did I dream that three months later we'd be walking around the Kremlin.

For five days and nights I have stared and walked and wondered. It's a strange city. I missed the street signs, the hubbub of traffic, the colorful clothing, the billboards, and the neon gleaming in the night.

Yet, there is much that is the same: people trying to make a living, people trying to keep their families together. And kids, wonderful kids with great faces. It would be wonderful if some day their kids and our kids could grow up into a world that spoke the same language and respected the same things.

My writers. I wonder if they ever made it back? (NBC photo)

Right now the world is busy building a bomb for every letter in the alphabet. That cannot be the answer. But there must be one. We must find some plan for peaceful co-existence, so that human beings don't become obsolete. With these rather solemn words, we ended our Moscow TV show when it appeared in America.

If we had any doubts about doing a show from Russia, they were certainly dispelled by the tremendous reception. There was an avalanche of favorable mail.

The critics were most enthusiastic and we won the coveted Peabody and Sylvania awards. The show was repeated a year later on NBC and met with the same response.

My plane for Copenhagen was due to leave Moscow at noon. Mort and Bill took me to the airport. The sleek Russian jet was poised for take-off. As I started up the ramp, I turned to Mort and said, "Whatever you do, don't leave without the film."

The Owl stared at me through his glasses and said, "Bob, nobody knows what will happen in that lab. What if they don't release the film? How long do you want us to wait?"

"Just don't come home without it."

Unbelieving, Bill said, "Bob, I never thought you were the kind of man who would sacrifice two human lives for a television show."

"Well, now you know," I said as I walked into the plane.

And now, patient reader, you know, too!

CHAPTER FIFTEEN

THE FAR EAST REVISITED

Our Secretary of State rushed to the airport. The pilot said, "Where to?" The Secretary of State replied, "Any-place—we've got trouble all over."

I did that joke for the first time about fifteen years ago. It never had more impact than it does today.

Just before Christmas, 1962, the Perry Como show took off for Guantánamo in a double-barreled attack against the Castroites and the Beverly Hillbillies. Ed Sullivan and his commandos waded ashore in the second wave.

Our troupe boarded a MATS cargo jet and headed west on a course that was to take us to Japan, Korea, Viet Nam, Formosa, Okinawa, Guam, and the Philippines.

Three hours out, the Defense Department canceled our play-dates at Viet Nam. We had a tremendous cast. In addition to our regulars—the Stash, Pete Leeds, and Les Brown —we had Lana Turner, Janis Paige, Anita Bryant, and Amedee Chabot, our reigning Miss USA. The Defense Department felt that a show this size would draw tremendous audiences and in a combat area like Viet Nam, it constituted an unnecessary risk to us and to the troops.

We had to settle for a reduced schedule: ten days in which to fly twenty thousand miles and do seventeen shows. Practically a rest cure.

I settled back for a nap expecting to wake up in Tokyo. When I stepped off the plane they threw a lei around my neck. Either we had a very sick navigator, or a brand-new Tokyo.

There was a simple explanation. We'd been bucking a hundred and ten mile headwind and we were running low on kerosene. The pilot had turned down the wick and headed for Honolulu.

I called my good friend General Emmett "Rosie" O'Donnell to say "Hi." Always a hospitable man, he invited me up for lunch. I asked him if I could bring a few friends and he, of course, agreed.

I hi-jacked a bus and ten minutes later, I was at his front door with the plane crew, the camera crew, the cast and the band. It was a second Pearl Harbor.

We polished off the turkey, the ham, the potato salad, the Scotch, the bourbon, the corn flakes, two candy canes and, for dessert, the band ate the bowl of wax fruit.

Leaving Rosie with little more than the four stars on his shoulders, we returned to our plane and started out once more for Tokyo.

The drive from the Tokyo International Airport to the hotel was a revelation. I was delighted to see that the Japanese had finally done something about their traffic problem. What a wonderful solution—driving on top of each other.

Actually, there isn't room to drive any place else. All the main roads are ripped up and being rebuilt as part of the preparation for the 1964 Olympic Games.

Keeping up "face" is a big thing in the Far East and the city of Tokyo has certainly gone all out. It may be the Land of the Rising Sun but nobody's going to see it with all the new skyscrapers.

We stayed at the Okura Hotel, just one of a score of new luxury hotels which awaits the transient transistor buyers.

I had a lovely suite. I hope to go back and see it some time. We spent our two days in helicopters flying to do shows at Tachikawa Air Base, Iwakuni Marine Base, and Atsugi Naval Base.

We ran into the original cast of Flower Drum Song *at the Marine Base, Iwakuni, Japan. (NBC photo by Herb Ball)*

Our schedule was so frantic that we only had a half hour for shopping. The cast made a mad scramble for the radios, tape recorders, and cameras. I bought Dolores a lovely string of genuine pearls for only seven dollars. I think they were genuine. The oyster had an honest face.

We switched to a prop plane for our hop to Korea. The runways from here on in couldn't handle the big jet job.

And I'm one guy who likes plenty of parking space. One thing I hate is an airplane with bent curb-feelers.

At Seoul, we were hustled to Hartell House in the Yong-san Compound where we were to be quartered for the next three nights.

We received a lengthy briefing from Navy Lieutenant Frank Poyet. He explained the rather complex monetary system. He warned us not to drink the water or eat any fresh vegetables off the base. And finally, he warned us to be sure and keep our luggage locked at all times. It was too late. By the time he warned us, our luggage was missing. And I had a claim against the insurance company for a thousand-dollar pearl necklace.

The following morning, I was rudely awakened by two MPs. I thought I'd been drafted. I had. To play golf with the commanding general, Guy S. Meloy, and two other generals on his staff, General Palmer and General Thatcher. This was really All-Star Golf.

We played a very pleasant straw-colored pasture, which is maintained for the guys who are rotated back from the 38th Parallel.

Golf is a wonderful recreation for the guys at these lonely bases. It gives them something to do instead of thinking about what they really want to do.

Like Japan, they have girl caddies in Korea. They understand the game very well and I like the way they keep score. I did very well that day, for eighteen holes. I shot a 両で. Pretty good for a man my age. My age is せ気.

The Sixth Transport Company banana coptered us all over Korea. They took us to the ASCOM area where we played a baseball field for 6000 Army, Air Force, and Marines. The next morning we sweated out the fog for three hours, so the copters could find their way into Osan. We were about to get on buses when the sun finally came through. Here, we played mostly to Air Force and some

At Schoonover Bowl (formerly Bayonet Bowl). They called me "Mama-san"—I'd better go on a diet. (NBC photo by Herb Ball)

Army. They came from Pusan, Kunson, and Taegu, as far as 300 miles away.

Our trip up to Schoonover Bowl was like old home week for us. When we last played it in 1957 it was called Bayonet Bowl. I recalled vividly the guys sitting up in the snow watching our show. What a fantastic audience those poor frozen kids had been. So this year I came prepared for this type of weather with a few crunchers like:

"It gets so cold here they use brass monkeys as hand warmers.

"I sneezed last night and my nose shattered.

"Don't stare . . . I had to put it together in the dark."

When I stepped out of the copter, I disappeared in the mud. There wasn't any snow on the ground. The sun was out, the sky was clear and the temperature was a balmy sixty-five.

I raced backstage and called for Barney McNulty so he could change the idiot cards. Barney was late. He didn't show up until two minutes before show time. When he finally staggered into my dressing tent I was all set to chew him out. But he stopped me cold.

"Sorry I'm late, Bob," said Barney, "but I had to buy back my idiot cards from the natives. They were using them to build houses."

I knew it was a lie, but it was such a good one that I gave him back his passport.

I walked out on the stage wearing the Papa-san hat and carrying a long thin pipe. The guys loved it and we ad-libbed back and forth until they got clever. They were a wonderful audience and we used that monologue to open our television show.

We also used a stand-up spot with Lana Turner. Lana was very nervous about appearing in front of a live audience. And, believe me, when they saw Lana they were live. She needn't have worried for a minute. I took three bows on her applause.

That night we played a second show. This one was at Collier field house for the Strategic Air Command. It wasn't until eleven P.M. that night that our hungry cast and crew finally sat down for our annual Christmas Eve dinner.

Usually at this dinner we exchange gifts. It's not a big production. We just draw names out of a hat and buy something that might get a laugh.

One of our loyal production gals, Onnie Morrow, had heard that a Salvation Army warehouse in Seoul had burned down and that an immense amount of clothing that was to

Panmunjom—The Christmas tree the Reds called a capitalistic weapon. (NBC photo by Herb Ball)

be given to the orphans had been destroyed. So instead of exchanging gifts, Onnie passed the hat and we all tossed in a few won. It was a small gesture on our part, a spur of the moment thing. Three weeks after our return to the States we received a magnificent letter of thanks.

Christmas morning we were issued special passes and badges to visit the Demilitarized Zone in Panmunjom. Judging from the map it should have been a simple straight flight. For a while I thought our copter pilot was an ex-Greyhound driver. He not only followed every curve on the road below us but he never even crossed the white line.

I asked the pilot why he didn't fly directly to Panmunjom. He had a pretty good explanation,

"We follow the road below in case we have to make an emergency landing. The area on both sides of the road is heavily mined."

I tightened my safety belt and crossed two more fingers.

We landed at Hotel No. 128 which is the designation for the helipad at the Joint Security Area. There we were greeted by various members of the United Nations party, including American, Swiss, Swedish, and South Korean officials.

The North Koreans and their Czech and Polish representatives were not on the helipad to greet us. However, the Red sentries watched us from their pagoda topped sentry boxes on the hill.

Our escort officers showed us the conference hut where the weekly truce talks were held. Everything is supposed to be identical on both sides of the table and on the table itself. We were shown one very interesting thing—the North Korean flagpole is one quarter-inch taller than the United Nations flagpole. The North Koreans insisted on it.

We walked freely back and forth across the demarcation line which runs through the exact center of the zone. As we walked along the road, two Red sentries came down the hill toward us. I turned and walked toward them. They retreated.

Then a Czechoslovakian general came down the hill toward us and walked over and shook hands. The United Nations party were amazed. This was a new high in sociability in the Security Area.

The general and I had a bit of a language problem but all was very cordial until I asked him if I might inspect the Red sentry box.

The general stiffened and replied, "It is not my matter. I have heard about your visit and I am pleased to meet you. That is all." He turned abruptly and walked off.

Being snubbed by the Commie guards at Panmunjom. Even Neilsen couldn't help my rating here. (NBC photo by Herb Ball)

At noon we flew back down a few miles south of the zone and had lunch at the enlisted men's mess at Camp Casey. There was quite a bit of excitement when Lana, Janis, Anita, and Amedee got in line with the guys for chow. The metal trays were piled high with a delicious turkey dinner. The gals ate heartily. The guys just stared. Meanwhile, Jerry, Les, Peter, and I sat in the corner eating humble pie. There are very few male celebrities in an Army camp.

After lunch we did a big show for the men of the 1st Cavalry Division at a football field near Yonjiko. I had a lot of trouble with that name but the audience was a pleasure. In addition to the eight thousand men were fifty Korean orphans who were our special guests. These kids are fed, clothed, and educated with money donated by the men of the 1st Cavalry. The GIs were very generous in their applause for us. I wish there was some way I could lead a little applause for them.

Also in the audience was a solemn little boy who wore the emblem of NBC on his sweater. He is the ward of our engineering and technical crews at NBC in Burbank. They support him with the profits from their coffee canteen.

It was impossible to reach as many guys in Korea as we hoped to in the short time we had. It's lonely duty and there is practically no entertainment. We tried something new. Christmas night we did our regular show for the Eighth Army at Collier field house near Yongsan. At the same time the entire show was telecast over a special closed-circuit hookup to remote outposts all over Korea. When I'm in a country there's no place to hide.

I did a lot of material that brought the guys up to date on happenings back home. Jokes about television, about Zsa Zsa getting married, about China and India, the newspaper strike in New York and what they liked most of all—jokes about their Commander-in-Chief.

"It's been a slow year back home. Only one Kennedy got elected.

"The Kennedys had a nice Christmas. Jackie got a new pair of water skiis. The President got a pair of hair clippers and Ted got a nice present . . . Massachusetts.

"I'm only kidding. There was a wonderful Christmas spirit in Washington this year. The Kennedys held a drive, 'Toys for Republicans.'

"Can you picture Christmas at the White House? Santa slides down the chimney and the FBI grabs him for breaking and entering.

Korean orphan sponsored by our NBC engineers in Hollywood. (NBC photo by Herb Ball)

Caroling with the cast and guards up in the Demilitarized Zone on Christmas Day. (NBC photo by Herb Ball)

"Then Jimmy Hoffa pickets the reindeer for carrying freight without a Teamsters' card."

From there on, we hopped around pretty good. In Formosa we played the City Hall Theatre for our Military Assistance and Advisory Group. That was a frantic show. Lana lost her voice and had to whisper her act. Colonna drove me on stage in a Taiwan pedicab. It's kind of a mixed up bicycle turned rickshaw with a mind of its own. The next thing I knew we were headed out over the footlights.

Amazing the crowd you can gather when it's free. (NBC photo by Herb Ball)

Everywhere the cast went in Taipei they were mobbed by the most frenzied fans I've ever seen. Some of them even followed me into the washroom. Fortunately, Barney was in the next booth with the idiot cards.

At Subic Bay in the Philippines, we played on the flight deck of the carrier *Kitty Hawk*.

A few hours later, we were at Clark Field, where we played for 12,000 men in Bamboo Bowl. There wasn't time to load the equipment on and off the plane, so it was trucked down over 90 miles of very rough terrain. Somewhere along the way the sound equipment flipped out of the truck and was damaged considerably. They were still patching the P.A. system together when we started the show.

I don't know what the bump did to the amplifier, but during the first three minutes of the show, I sounded like Yma Sumac.

Before taking off for Guam, we paid a quick visit to the Negrito village. We were greeted by the chief or general, as he was called. He invited me to inspect the troops who stood there in loin cloths, holding spears and blowguns. All we needed was Anita Ekberg and it would have looked like a production number from my latest picture, *Call Me Bwana*.

They live in simple straw huts on poles. They wear cast off clothing from the base and make a meager living selling feather trimmed spears to the occasional tourist who might happen by. Yet, these primitive, pigmy head-hunters are savage, loyal fighters. They saved us 75 days in the recapture of the Philippines. They are experts at psychological warfare. At night, they would slip behind the enemy lines and slit the throat of every other man.

I don't know why they're wasting their time in the Philippine jungle. They'd make a fortune in Hollywood as agents.

Our last stop was at what was left of Guam. I was their second big wind of the year. Only the heavy fellows were left. But that was quite a few. The audience filled the big hanger at Agana Naval Air Station and was seated all the way out to the runway.

As we were about to board our C-135 jet and take-off for home, our Project Officer Major Ed Swinney came up and whispered to me, "Bob, the starter on engine number four is broken. We'll start engine number one then transfer the starter to engine number four and get it started. But for heaven's sake, don't tell the others."

And I didn't. I tried to, but I couldn't make my mouth move.

Right after this the Negritos put the apple back on my head. (NBC photo by Herb Ball)

We hit thunderstorms all the way home. It was a rough flight but the big bump came when we hit customs in Los Angeles. They were pretty easy on me but some of the cast and crew were two and a half hours getting through. I was plenty aggravated and a little tired, I guess. Anyway, I popped off pretty good to the press. Then as I was riding home in the car, it hit me. What was I mad about? Just 48 hours ago in Okinawa, I'd been on stage. In the audience were litter patients, guys who were just off the ambulance planes from the tough fighting in Viet Nam. I had looked down and noticed that one of the guys was getting a plasma transfusion. And he was laughing at a joke I was telling.

That sight paid off everybody in our show. It was a great reason for anybody making one of these trips to entertain. How could this trip be bad? Flying twenty thousand miles on the same plane with Lana Turner, Janis Paige, Anita Bryant, and the gorgeous Miss USA. I'd just like to catch the sneak who locked me in the washroom.